Everyone Is Getting Off On Mr. Skin!

"I have nothing but love for Mr. Skin. They celebrate female nudity on film/tv and never say anything mean!! What's not to love?"

—ANNA PAQUIN

"I no longer have to waste valuable time with 'plot.' More than just a time-saver, Mr. Skin may have saved my life."

—JIMMY KIMMEL

"Thank you so much! I am so honored. *L'chaim!*"

—SARAH SILVERMAN, after receiving a Mr. Skin Anatomy Award

"Wow. What can I even say? To all the men who've ever turned me down...now all you can do is look at photos and cry the salty tears of regret. It's truly an honor. Thank you for your support."

—ALEXANDRA DADDARIO, after winning Mr. Skin
2017 Whack-It-Bracket

"For me, the best part of Mr. Skin on *The Howard Stern Show* is his delightful accent. Makes me feel like I'm at the food court at the Woodfield mall."

—ANDY RICHTER

"Mr. Skin knows more about nudity in movies than any person who ever lived has ever known about any subject. Ever."

—RICHARD ROEPER

BEING MR. SKIN

20 YEARS OF NIP SLIPS, CHEEK PEEKS, AND FAST-FORWARDING TO THE GOOD PARTS

JIM "MR. SKIN" McBRIDE
WITH MATHEW KLICKSTEIN

Post Hill
PRESS

A POST HILL PRESS BOOK

Being Mr. Skin:
20 Years of Nip Slips, Cheek Peeks, and Fast-Forwarding
to the Good Parts
© 2019 by Jim "Mr. Skin" McBride with Mathew Klickstein
All Rights Reserved

ISBN: 978-1-64293-032-0
ISBN (eBook): 978-1-64293-033-7

Cover art by Cody Corcoran
Interior design and production, Greg Johnson, Textbook Perfect

Post Hill Press
New York • Nashville
posthillpress.com

Published in the United States of America

CONTENTS

FOREWORD

Do we really need a book about Mr. Skin, the "World's Premiere Celebrity Nudity Expert"? Read on for my answer.

Mr. Skin and I are approximately the same age, members of the generation of men between forty-five and a million who grew up waiting for *Barbarella* or any Russ Meyer movie—nay, film—to come onto cable at midnight on a Saturday evening. (Not that the Carollas had cable; I'd have to go to a friend's house whose parents weren't losers). Even an episode of *Benny Hill* would do.

Imagine you're thirteen in the late 1970s, desperately praying that this particular *Benny Hill* episode you're watching alone on a Zenith TV that was deeper than it was wide while everyone else is asleep might offer a quick glimpse of a scantily-clad British bird in the changing room at the beach.

It was fucking pathetic. Especially since our faces would be shoved against the screen for a half hour to catch a hummingbird's heartbeat of boobie. But it was all guys like Mr. Skin and I had back then.

I *have* a thirteen-year-old boy. One day I'll sit him down for a father-son discussion and explain that there was a time when there was no Pornhub and YouPorn and YouJizz and god knows whatever he's typing into his Google "Incognito" window. Nope, there was a time when Dad would have to go out into a field and lie on his back and wait until the cloud took the shape of a tit.

That was all we had. Then Mr. Skin came into our lives.

The first time Mr. Skin came onto my radio show, being that we're about the same age, we bonded over the movies and TV shows we both scanned like the Zapruder film for the hint of a nipple. I found him to be encyclopedic, and nearly autistic, in his recall of movies, ass cracks, and side boobs.

It's this knowledge and Rain Man recall of celebrity nudity that is impressive to a certain portion of the population. I would include myself in that group. It's probably just as nauseating to the remaining majority of other human beings who roam the planet.

Which brings us right back to where we started. Since most people wouldn't necessarily care about Mr. Skin or probably even know he exists, do we need this book you're about to read?

Look, this foreword is by a guy who's written *four* books. And the world didn't need any books from Adam Carolla. So, I'd be a hypocrite if I said the world doesn't need anyone *else's* either.

We live in a world where everyone from Paris Hilton to Bob Denver has written a book about themselves. I would say, then, that if Mr. Skin's book falls somewhere in between *The Catcher in the Rye* and one of the *Real Housewives of Orange County*'s tell-all tomes, then, yes, we may not *need* his book and we may not even *want* his book. But that's the beauty of this country: Mr. Skin gets to foist one on us whether we like it or not. God Bless America.

—*Adam Carolla*

SKINTRODUCTION

Portrait of the World's Foremost Authority on Celebrity Nudity as a Young Man...plus his haircut. This is my seventh grade yearbook pic from 1976, the same year *Bobbie Jo and the Outlaw* came out, featuring Lynda Carter (aka TV's Wonder Woman) in the nude. You got your education, I got mine.

November 9, 1980. Sunday morning. 6:00 a.m.

I'm a teenager and I'm tiptoeing downstairs like a kindergartener on Christmas morning—the sneaky kid who's hoping to unwrap whatever booty Santa left behind before anybody else wakes up.

Key words there: "unwrap" and "booty."

Elsewhere in the house, my parents and three younger sisters snooze obliviously. Perfect.

Outside, it's River Forest, Illinois. My hometown. More importantly, it's also one of the first Chicago-area suburbs to get cable TV. More important than that still, my dad—whose snoring I'm keeping half an ear on to make sure he stays unconscious—raced to be an early adapter in the dawn-of-the-decade home entertainment revolution.

As a result, Clan McBride not only boasted fully loaded cable TV service with every premium movie channel (HBO, Showtime, Cinemax, and a local obscurity called TK), we owned *two* Betamax videotape-recording machines.

In 1980 terms, this equipment put us in the future. It also put me down in the TV room that day before the sun came up, an adolescent

3

on an antsy mission: keep quiet, gather the goods, and maintain cool in the face of more unclothed female anatomy than I could eyeball in six months of pilfered *Playboys*—and these bodies came in glorious motion picture form, to boot!

I had devised a full-fledged, patented system to (ab)use my weekly channel guide that accidentally clued me in on which films had those golden nuggets of nudity in them. I could then set up my video recorder to tape these particular films, leaving me with a treasure trove of goodies to watch the following morning while everyone else was asleep.

First up on the fast-forward roster was *The Kentucky Fried Movie*, an outrageous sketch comedy revue I hadn't really heard of.

Nine minutes into *KFM*, my finger not only backed off the FF button, I think I hit a second puberty on the spot. During a parody preview titled "Catholic High School Girls in Trouble," the most volcanically voluptuous beauty I'd ever seen converted my TV into a "boob tube" beyond anything I could have imagined (and I imagined *plenty*).

In the course of the bit, this superhumanly endowed knockout takes a shower with the luckiest pair of hands in the history of show business, as those mitts massage her basketball-proportioned appendages while accompanied by comical balloon squeak sound effects. *National Lampoon*: eat your heart out!

Then, during a blip of simulated sex, the spectacularly stacked siren bounces her massive mammaries repeatedly against the semi-steamy glass shower door.

Somehow, a moment of clarity struck me: I thought about how my prankster high school pals would moon each other up against a window and call it a "pressed ham." Watching in wonder, then, I whispered: "Pressed mams!"

In that instant—I mean, "skinstant"—I first combined movie nudity with merciless wordplay and, right there, set off on my "mam"-ifest destiny. One more element would complete the package: obsessive attention to detail and authoritative mastery of the bare facts.

In the course of building my lascivious video library, I'd pour myself into researching my favorite naked starlets and make notes in hope of tracking them down in any other unclad productions.

So while *The Kentucky Fried Movie* contained other (T&)A-plus nude scenes, let's focus, now, on that particularly hefty-chested Catholic High School Girl in Trouble.

Her name was Uschi Digard. I learned that she was a Swedish fetish model best known worldwide for her work with Russ Meyer—a filmmaker who specialized in over-the-top(less) sexploitation flicks that featured the most naturally bazooka-busted women ever photographed.

That knowledge prompted me to be on the lookout for any cable showings of Russ Meyer classics, as well as to head straight for his tapes among the racks at the countless video rental shops that began cropping up everywhere.

At the same time, I put together that another Russ Meyer glamazon, Francesca "Kitten" Natividad, had flashed her upper anatomy forty-seven minutes into the mainstream blockbuster farce *Airplane!*—a flick that was made, in turn, by the three guys who wrote *The Kentucky Fried Movie*, which, in another turn, was directed by John Landis, who also helmed the flesh-drenched comedy classic *Animal House*.

So, yes, while my devotion had much to do with erections, it was also profoundly about connections.

Let's get back to the Sunday morning at (one free) hand, though. After *The Kentucky Fried Movie* finished, 1979's *H.O.T.S.* came up next in the fast-forward queue. It's a nutty campus frolic that existed solely to showcase nudity (and, okay, to provide hilariously awkward leading man work to grown-up *Partridge Family* kid Danny Bonaduce).

H.O.T.S. starred an array of *Playboy* Playmates and, as likely comes as no surprise, I recognized each one as she appeared on screen and scribbled down exactly what she showed and when.

Following *H.O.T.S.* was *Slap Shot*, a bawdy, brawling Paul Newman hockey epic from 1977 that I was actually too young to see when it played in theaters. Now I was seeing it all—namely, what lay at the twenty-nine-minute mark where Melinda Dillon bares her breasts in bed next to Newman.

"Hold on!" I thought. "I know her! That's the mom from *Close Encounters of the Third Kind!*"

Indeed, not only had Melinda starred in Steven Spielberg's 1977 sci-fi smash, a few years onward, I would stun friends during annual

FIVE FAVORITE TV MOMS WHO HAVE GOTTEN NUDE

From tit-coms to reality TV T&A, a salute to mommies rearest!

5. **Jane Kaczmarek** (Lois, *Malcolm in the Middle*) in *Wildly Available* (0:29)

4. **Edie Falco** (Carmela Soprano, *The Sopranos*) in *Firehouse* (0:28)

3. **Felicity Huffman** (Lynette Scavo, *Desperate Housewives*) in *Transamerica* (1:34)

2. **Joanna Kerns** (Maggie Seaver, *Growing Pains*) in *The Nightman* (0:45)

1. **Meredith Baxter** (Elyse Keaton, *Family Ties*) in *My Breast* (0:16)

yuletide reruns of *A Christmas Story*, as Melinda plays the mother in that 1983 classic, too.

Amidst all the Red Ryder BB gun shenanigans, I'd inform everyone within earshot precisely where they could get a gander at Ralphie's mom's thoroughly a-peel-ing banana-shaped boobs.

So, on that stunning Sunday morning, those three "N"-blessed productions proved to be the triple crown of things to come in my life, my career, and my overall purpose on a planet full of naked actresses.

Sticking to the mission, then, I transferred the scenes between Betamaxes, scrawled copious notes, and rushed back upstairs.

From there, I moved on to my next assignment: showering and getting ready for church. The McBrides attended 9:30 a.m. mass at St. Luke's every Sunday and—at least in that sense—this one would be no different.

March 6, 2018. Tuesday morning. 7:00 a.m.

I flew to New York to promote Mr. Skin's 19th Annual Anatomy Awards on the mightiest mecca of all radio destinations, *The Howard Stern Show*.

Since 2000, Howard has invited me into the studio every year to run through my annual parody of the Academy Awards. It's an honor, a privilege, a riotous good time—and also a massive source of stress for me, as I always want to properly rise to the occasion (pun, for once, not intended).

I'm a fanatical devotee of Howard Stern and have listened religiously for decades. For that reason, I put a lot of pressure on myself each Anatomy Awards season to live up to his standards.

With the Anatomy Awards, I get to talk to Howard, Robin, and the gang each year about the most prominent celebrity nude scenes of the previous twelve months and announce my pick for Breast Picture.

Howard is the world's funniest, most skilled, and all around most amazing interviewer. Bar none. On top of that, he has a great time with what I do for a living, so much so that Howard has immeasurably helped me turn what I do into a living—and a life—beyond my most ambitious dreams.

So, when I got back to Chicago after the 2018 Anatomy Awards, I breathed a sigh of relief and felt a massive amount of gratitude. That's the first thing on my mind as I wake up this morning. The second thing is breakfast.

With nine radio shows on the docket before 9:30 a.m., I take my one available break at 7:15 and step into the kitchen.

I hear, "Hi, Daddy!"

It's my ten-year-old daughter. She goes on, "Dad, are you coming to my art class open house this morning at ten?"

"You bet I'll be there," I say. "Now can you grab a brush and get started on your hair?"

"Daaaad," she moans, reaching for a hairbrush anyway. She then asks if I'll make her some toast.

"Of course!" I say. "Two toasty slices coming right up. Can you pass the butt hair?"

"Dad," she says, "your jokes are so bad, they're not even jokes!"

I'm glad Howard Stern doesn't agree with her. Still, I smile and get cooking. I do it every day. My daughter likes toast. My other daughter eats fruit and cereal. My twelve-year-old sports-loving son downs sausage and eggs. For myself, it's an egg white omelet.

Mrs. Skin—Michelle—passes by on her way out the door. She's got to get to work early and she'll pick something up. We kiss goodbye.

After packing lunches, signing permission slips, and getting the kids off to school, I settle back in for the next nonstop round of Anatomy Awards promos.

As I write this in 2018, Mr. Skin continues to rise and shine. I am the World's Foremost Authority on Celebrity Nudity and my family's foremost authority on being a husband, dad, and short-order breakfast cook.

I didn't plan on any of this but, looking back, I did everything in my power to make it all happen—one naked movie star, one hit radio appearance, and one incredible, loving family at a time.

FOREPLAY

ORIGINS AND SKINFINING MOMENTS

Hard at Work

As I do with my website, I'm going to have some fun with this book. But I'm also going to be completely honest with you as I reveal how I got from *there* to *here*. Something that comes up in a lot of my interviews and radio shows is a good place to start: *Is being Mr. Skin the best job in the world?*

It sure *seems* like the best job—to me, my staff of almost fifty people, and my friends and family who have been so supportive while I built and continue to maintain MrSkin.com, the internet's premier database of celebrity nudity for two decades running.

True, that last line's what our PR hype material reads. It really is the case, though. I've got the torrential web traffic and loyal audience to prove it. Twenty million monthly visits and forty-five million monthly page views across our network of websites place us among the highest-trafficked sites on the web.

How many times can one man be called "the World's Foremost Authority on Celebrity Nudity" by media outlet after media outlet before he has to sit back and admit it: "You know what? I guess that's me!"

I've been doing this for twenty unbelievable years. I've endured a few minor mishaps, learned a few important lessons—both in business and life—and, mostly, enjoyed a lot more laughs. As my company president and close friend Sam would say, "It's been an interesting ride."

You'll see how interesting as you continue reading this book that I never thought I'd be writing. Certainly not when I first started being Mr. Skin back in the late nineties.

That's *nineteen*-nineties for all you ragamuffin millennials out there who might not be aware that there was a world before BuzzFeed and Huffington Post and even—yes—Facebook, Twitter, and Google. That's right: you used to have to look up information in *books* or—*gasp*—go to the library to find out, say, who played bodacious, buxom Betty in *Revenge of the Nerds*. (Answer: Julia Montgomery, who did the mamorable topless scene at the 0:49 minute mark of that skin classic.)

And if you wanted to find a *picture* of her, well, you might be SOL.

Which is where I came in.

What I wanted to do with this newfangled thing I had only recently heard about called a "website" was help out all of the guys (and gals) like me who have a passion for celebrity nudity. I wanted my site to be the ultimate one-stop shop for fans who needed a safe, well-researched, and cleanly crafted place online where they could explore all the photos, clips, and write-ups they could handle about their favorite naked stars from the big and small screens.

Here I am today. The dream has become a reality. I've become Mr. Skin, the superintendent of the most complete database for celebrity nudity online. And, I'd wager, anywhere else. Yup, we do have printed Skincyclopedias out there...and you can find plenty of copies being passed around some of our nation's finest correctional institutions.

Being the CSO (chief sexecutive officer) and founder of a website and company like Mr. Skin, leading fifty employees who work their asses off day and night—many of them for almost as long as I've been here myself—is something that I can't believe is actually my life.

A lot of it's been luck. No doubt about it. I told you that I'm going to be as forthright as possible in this book, and if that's the case (hint: it is), I must own up to that conspicuous fact. Man, I *have* been really, *really* lucky.

Yeah, it's been a lot of hard work. You don't get to a position like this without rolling up your sleeves, sacrificing, and doing whatever you have to do to make it happen. But I never planned any of this. I don't know *how* you could plan this out, how you could plan to become Mr. Skin.

A lot of the luck was about timing. Being in the right place at the right time with the right idea that—who would've thought?—could work. A lot of the luck was about knowing the right folks or being introduced to the right folks or, in one particularly fateful situation, being at the right bar when tapped on the shoulder by the right guy.

So, here's the *really* big question. Probably the main reason you picked up and bought this book. Or clicked on its cover image and purchased it from Amazon. *How the hell did I become Mr. Skin?*

There were three defining moments I can point to as my answer. Whether it was luck, or hard work, or relationships I cultivated, or the innate ability that people in the past have referred to as my Rain

Man–like memory for celebrity nudity information, these "Skinfining Moments" are what led to it all happening over my twenty-year quixotic quest to be who and where I am today.

My lovely, beautiful, and supportive wife Michelle would tell you that it was *I* who made these moments so very Skinfining. (Though, she probably wouldn't use that exact word. She's a highly respected attorney and doesn't talk like that. Most of the time, she thinks my use of these goofy words are merely further evidence of my being a cornball.)

But, she's right: I had to do all I could to take advantage of these three very special circumstances that came up as I constructed my company. Without me, MrSkin.com would have never gotten off the ground. And it could never have skyrocketed into becoming the online empire it's exploded into. Or, should I say, *Skin*pire. (Sorry, Michelle.)

WHAT WAS THE "FIRST" CELEBRITY NUDE SCENE?

The answer will surprise you, and that's a promise. (Promise! Promise!)

There were a few dalliances with nudity onscreen in the earliest days of cinema. (O, those wily Europeans!) We're talking here about Eadweard Muybridge's academic study short subject "The Human Figure in Motion—Descending the Stairs and Turning Around" (1884), Albert Kirchner's blue-tinted, seven-minute short "Bedtime for the Bride" (1896), and (perhaps cinema's greatest magician of all time) Georges Méliès' "After the Ball, After the Bath" (1896). The last of which is considered by many to be the world's first "adult film."

At just under a minute and ten seconds long, Méliès' film was marketed as "being suitable for private screenings to broad-minded bachelors."

As far as *celebrity* nudity is concerned, it's a T&A technicality, but the very first commercial motion picture to intentionally showcase a mainstream celebrity's bare breasts is a lost obscurity titled *A Daughter of the Gods*. It's a silent undersea fantasy saga starring well-known real-life swimming champion Annette Kellermann as a mermaid who does flash her naked torso flippers a few times.

In terms of vintage vixens who sent contemporary movie nudity in forward motion, though, the first celebrity nude scene of the modern era belongs to blonde bombshell Jayne Mansfield, who busts out her jugs repeatedly in the raunchy sex farce, *Promises! Promises!*.

Prior to going bare on the big screen, Jayne ruled the 1950s as the main curvaceous competition to Marilyn Monroe as Hollywood's hottest sex goddess.

After Marilyn died in the course of making what was supposed to be her own debut nude scene in the unfinished film *Something's Got to Give*, Jayne took up the T&A mantle and splashed herself naked across movie screens.

As a result, *Promises! Promises!* is the first film of the sound era to feature a mainstream star nude on screen. It's also the first flick to sell itself on that very fact by touting the tagline: "You read about her in *Playboy* Magazine... Now see *all* of Jayne Mansfield!"

In another first, *Promises* promoted itself with nude photos of Jayne on the set that ran in the July 1963 issue of *Playboy*—a spread that prompted a Chicago obscenity bust that became the only time publisher Hugh Hefner ever got arrested. He later beat the rap.

Critics panned *Promises*, but the public devoured every naked bit of it. The movie made so much money that the National Association of Theater Owners voted Jayne one of the Top 10 Box Office Attractions of the Year.

While almost entirely forgotten now, *Promises! Promises!* will forever hold reign as the movie that made celebrity nude scenes possible—and Mr. Skin the man he is today (and forever!).

Skin the Beginning

It was 1975.

I was thirteen years old. Home was the Chicago suburbs, as you'll recall. I still live there today.

My hormones were raging, and I was thinking about girls nonstop. Did I mention I was a *thirteen-year-old boy*?

When I would turn on the TV, there would be these outrageously gorgeous actresses dolled up in short-shorts and miniskirts, painted radiantly in colorful makeup, with just incredible hairstyles. Did I mention yet that this was 1975?

I couldn't help but fall in love over and over again—wholesome and blonde Marcia Brady on *The Brady Bunch*; the dark-haired Laurie Partridge; Rosalie "Hotsy" Totsy on *Welcome Back, Kotter*; and who could forget the original girls-next-door, Julie and Barbara Cooper on Norman Lear's *One Day at a Time*.

Now, here was the problem. Remember the whole "it being 1975" thing? If you grew up in the seventies as I did, your options for boobs and butts onscreen were few and far between.

It was nearly *impossible* to see naked women onscreen back then. Especially if you were some dumb kid living in the 'burbs. You turned on the television (yeah, you actually had to go up to your big ol' wooden-framed set in your living room and *turn the knobs*) and your choices were hopelessly limited to CBS, NBC, and ABC. It was nothing like it is today where you don't even *need* a remote to navigate all the nudity your rapidly beating little heart desires online, on your phone, on your smart TV, or in any number of easily purchased, deliverable niche print publications.

What did I do to satiate my perfectly healthy carnal cravings? It wasn't unheard of for me to take a Sears catalog to my bedroom and delight in the bra ads. There was also the occasional *National Geographic* magazine that might have some nubile native nudity in it. Otherwise, I was left with a depressing dearth of nakedness.

All of this is to say that if you were a thirteen-year-old boy in the middle of the seventies and you wanted to look at nudity, you were screwed. And not in the good way. It was brutal, man.

Hello, My Lovelies

Let's fast-forward to fall, 1980. I'm a senior in high school.

Suddenly, the clouds opened up and the sun shined through. The bright, vivifying illumination of what would become a perfect lightning storm of technology broke through the staid gray. I'm talking here of the convergence of the two goddamn *greatest* things that happened in my life up to that point: this was that glorious time when my dad got us cable television, and we got a Betamax.

For those wondering, "What the hell's a Betamax?"—the answer to all my imploring boyish prayers. A Betamax was a magical machine that allowed you to *record* what you saw on TV. This was before there was such a device as the later VCR. And after we got our *first* Betamax, my dad was compassionate enough to take pity on his über-horny son and—*praise the heavens*—buy us a *second* Betamax. Which is more important than you'd think, and I'll get into the reason why in a second.

Meanwhile, I can't sit here today, tremblingly writing these words, and properly express to you the shock and awe of what it meant to first turn on cable television. HBO, Showtime, Cinemax. There they all were, at my fingertips: raunchy British sex comedies, raunchy *Italian* sex comedies, women-in-prison movies, uninhibited blaxploitation films, sexy slasher movies…all *loaded* with top-shelf female nudity. Full-frontal, even!

I never wanted to leave the house again.

I taped it all on my Betamax. As many movies as I could.

What I would do—*oh, what a clever boy am I!*—was scan through the cable guide and find any movie that had a big black "N" next to its title. This was the *good* "'N' word," the one that meant "nudity." I'd high-light the film title and, that evening, would set up my Betamax to tape two, three, or four films.

TOP FIVE PG-MOVIE NUDE SCENES

Parental Guidance Suggested—because members of the audience might get erected!

5. **Kitten Natividad**—*Airplane!* (0:47)
4. **Darryl Hannah**—*Splash* (0:27)
3. **JoBeth Williams**—*Kramer vs. Kramer* (0:44)
2. **Elizabeth McGovern**—*Ragtime* (0:52)
1. **Tanya Roberts**—*Sheena* (0:54)

TOP FIVE PG-13 NUDE SCENES

Between PG and R, classic T&A.

5. **Milla Jovovich**—*The Fifth Element* (0:27)
4. **Kate Winslet**—*Titanic* (1:25)
3. **Julie Warner**—*Doc Hollywood* (0:16)
2. **Joyce Hyser**—*Just One of the Guys* (1:28)
1. **Kelly LeBrock**—*The Woman in Red* (1:14)

THE STRIP!: MOVIE RATINGS

EVER WONDER WHY MOVIES ARE GIVEN RATINGS LIKE G, PG, PG-13, R AND THE EVER-CHANGING X/NC-17?

ALMOST IMMEDIATELY AFTER THE DEVELOPMENT OF CINEMA, THERE WERE ISSUES WITH CENSORSHIP...

AS A REACTION TO THIS, THE NEW YORK BOARD OF MOTION PICTURE CENSORSHIP WAS FORMED IN 1909...

THE NAME WOULD BE CHANGED TO THE CURRENT ITERATION: THE NATIONAL BOARD OF REVIEW OF MOTION PICTURES!

THROUGHOUT THE MID-1900s, FILM PRODUCERS WOULD SUBMIT THEIR FILMS TO THE N.B.R. IN ORDER TO GAIN THE COVETED "PASSED BY THE NATIONAL BOARD OF REVIEW" LOGO FOR THEIR PICTURE'S OPENING CREDIT...

THIS WOULD MORE OR LESS PROTECT THE FILM FROM BEING DENIED SCREENING AT THEATERS!

STARTING IN 1930, THE MAJOR STUDIOS USED WHAT WAS KNOWN AS THE MOTION PICTURE PRODUCTION CODE AS A SET OF GUIDELINES TO GOVERN WHAT WAS AND WHAT WAS NOT CONSIDERED "OBJECTIONABLE" FOR THEATER OWNERS/GOERS...

BEING THAT THE HEAD OF THE MOTION PICTURE PRODUCERS + DISTRIBUTORS OF AMERICA DURING MUCH OF THIS PERIOD (1922-1945) WAS NAMED WILLIAM HAYS, THE SET OF GUIDELINES BECAME KNOWN AS THE HAYS CODE...

THE MPPDA ITSELF WOULD LATER BECOME KNOWN AS THE MOTION PICTURE ASSOCIATION OF AMERICA...

IN THE LATTER HALF OF THE 20th CENTURY DUE TO LESS LEGAL RESTRICTIONS AND CULTURAL SENSIBILITIES, THE HAYS CODE WAS REPLACED BY THE MODERN MPAA FILM RATINGS SYSTEM...

STARTING IN 1968, THESE RATINGS WERE "G" (GENERAL AUDIENCES) "M" (MATURE AUDIENCES)...

"R" (RESTRICTED / THOSE UNDER 17 MUST BE ACCOMPANIED BY AN ADULT), AND "X" (NO ADMITTANCE FOR PERSONS UNDER 17).

IN 1970, "M" WAS CHANGED TO "PG" (PARENTAL GUIDANCE)

BECAUSE "X" WAS THE ONLY RATING NOT TRADEMARKED BY THE MPAA, THE RISING PORNOGRAPHY INDUSTRY WAS ABLE TO CO-OPT THE RATING AS A KIND OF BADGE OF HONOR...

THEY WOULD GO ON TO UTILIZE MULTIPLE "X's" FOR RATINGS OF THEIR FILMS ("XXX", etc.) TO PUBLICLY HYPE THEIR PICTURES...

STEVEN SPIELBERG BECAME AWARE THAT HIS PG-RATED FILMS, SUCH AS 1977's 'JAWS', WERE NOT APPROPRIATE FOR YOUNGER VIEWERS.

HE SUGGESTED TO THE MPAA THAT THEY INSTITUTE A NEW "PG-14" RATING...

...WHICH THEY TOOK TO HEART TO CREATE THE NEW "PG-13" RATING...

MEANWHILE, THE ADULT FILM INDUSTRY'S MARKETING STRATEGY OF ALTERING THE PERCEPTION OF THE "X" RATING LED TO THE MPAA'S DOING AWAY WITH THEIR "X" RATING AND OPTING INSTEAD FOR THE "NC-17" (NO CHILDREN-UNDER 17) RATING IN 1990...

IN 1996, THE "NC-17" RATING WAS CHANGED TO DISALLOW ATTENDANCE IN THEATERS OF ANYONE UNDER 18...

I'd wake up in the morning and would bolt down the stairs to check out what I'd craftily recorded. I'd fast-forward straight away to the nude scenes. Or, what we've been calling at Mr. Skin for the past twenty years: *the good parts!*

Going back to my generous and loving father's purchase of a *second* Betamax, I'd take these "good parts" from the first tape and transfer them over to a *second* tape recording on my *other* Betamax.

I was making my own personal highlights reel. Only this wasn't the *Wide World of Sports.*

I became the kid with the five-hour videotapes of nude scenes. Before long, I had boxes and boxes (and boxes) of these highlight reels.

In the seventies, there was pretty much no one you wanted to see naked the way you wanted desperately to see Lynda Carter naked. Watching her as Wonder Woman on ABC sporting that red, white, and blue dominatrix outfit with her big boobs nearly poking out? Are you *kidding* me? For a boner-prone boy wonder back then, she was where it was at, for sure.

I'm rifling through my cable guide as usual one night, and there I find it: *Oh, my god!* It was a movie called *Bobbie Jo and the Outlaw.* Some random drive-in flick made in 1976. No one remembers it now, but it was one of the movies I made sure to record on my trusty Betamax that week.

I wake up bright and early the following morning, dash down to the TV room, rewind the tape, and dutifully fast-forward to the good parts. That's when I see it.

Man, oh, man! Lynda Freaking Carter! Wonder Woman herself, naked *three...whole...times!* In the first thirty-five minutes alone! It's all magnificently capped off with Carter popping some 'shrooms...while skinny-dipping...with some big Indian chief.

Holy geez.

Two years later, I hit the mother lode. You remember *The Dukes of Hazzard?* It was a southern-fried sitcom that was later turned into a movie with Johnny Knoxville, Stifler from *American Pie,* Burt Reynolds as Boss Hogg, and Jessica Simpson as a young lady those of us alive in the late seventies and early eighties remember only too well as Daisy Duke.

On the TV show, Daisy was played to perfection by an actress named Catherine Bach.

I soon got my wish. Turns out Bach was in a 1978 movie called *Crazed*, and at the hour-and-three-minute mark, there she is...*topless*. You better believe I had my *own* Boss Hogg when I saw that!

Then there was one actress I got to see the way God intended, who was *really* the Holy Grail. More wonderful than Wonder Woman. Sunnier than Daisy Duke. Who could I possibly mean? Marcia Brady herself.

You don't believe me? Adorably fresh-faced and winsome Marcia Brady naked in a movie? It happened. It was about four or five years after the Bunch got bumped off the air. The movie is called *Texas Lightning*, and despite any—hmm—faults with its freewheeling crafts-manship, I'm of course recording it anyway, thanks to that telltale "N" emblazoned next to its title in my cable guide, and it's Marcia, Marcia, Marcia: Maureen McCormick.

And Marcia, Marcia, Marcia is smoking, smoking, smoking ciga-rettes. She's swearing, swearing, swearing. She's drinking, drinking, drinking. And then...an hour and four minutes into this fun-filled flick that wasn't exactly an Oscar contender, Marcia's topless, topless, *top-less*. In a seedy motel room.

Just call me Sure-wood Schwartz!

Something that struck me as essential in my lifelong quest for nudity at this primordial stage was: Why was I fixated on *celebrity* nudity?

See, it's one thing to flip through a *Playboy* or a *Hustler* or some weirdo fetish magazine. Or, these days, more likely surfing through clips on Pornhub or RedTube.

It's another thing to watch *celebrity* nudity, to have a sense that you *know* the person you're watching in the flesh. There's a certain special amazement in that intimate moment.

It's why celebrity sex tapes and leaked phone pics always make such a massive media splash in the endless ocean of the net's nude pics and videos. It's the lure of celebrity itself.

As hot as anonymous nudity can be, it's more sex-citing to gaze on the nude female form of someone to whom we feel connected. We "know" them through their interviews and Twitter feeds. Some we take

FOREPLAY

to bed with us via their tell-all memoirs or documentaries on our boudoir televisions.

The comedian Robert Kelly had a great way of describing this appeal, of why people still come to my (pay) site even though the world is awash in free porn: "It's like being a kid and seeing your teacher at the store. It's jolting: 'Oh my god! She buys stuff?'"

It's why Meryl Streep flashing one second of boob in *Silkwood* can be more titillating than a twenty-minute *Playboy* video of a model taking a shower. We *know* Streep. We've seen her interviewed. We know who her husband is. We know who her daughter is.

The job of a celebrity is to create a personal connection that constantly leaves us wanting to follow them wherever they go, wanting to know more about their continuing career and life.

We can't help but be captivated by these celebrities and their passions, their social causes, their complicated dating lives. In ways we might not even be aware of, our allegiance to them helps define who *we* are.

Pop Goes the Eighties

We now find ourselves in the early eighties. I've got cable television. I've got not one but two Betamaxes. And it's the Golden Age of teen sex comedies.

You can read more about that in an upcoming compendium called *Teen Movie Hell* by my former head writer and longtime pal Mike "McBeardo" McPadden. More on *him* in a little while. (Trust me, it's worth the weight. I mean, wait.)

The years 1980 to 1985 really were the epoch of the best teen comedies ever made. It's no wonder to me that we can look forward to an entire book on the subject. Funny, great movies that also had *plenty* of fantastic nude scenes.

Porky's in 1982. The greatest group shower scene in the history of movies! Also, one of the funniest lines: "Enough wool to knit a sweater!"

My Tutor. Miss Caren Kaye's acting career didn't necessarily make the grade after this movie came out. But we can get schooled all we want by her playing a sultry tutor for lucky devil Matt Lattanzi in this

23

THE STRIP!

PARA-SOCIAL RELATION-SHIPS!

WHY DO PEOPLE CONNECT SO INTENTLY WITH CHARACTERS ON SCREEN?

POP CORN

EVER NOTICE HOW NEWS ANCHORS, TALK SHOW HOSTS AND OTHER PUNDITS ALWAYS TALK *DIRECTLY TO THE CAMERA?*

WHEN A PERSON ON TV OR IN A MOVIE BREAKS THE "FOURTH WALL" AND SEEMS TO BE SPEAKING DIRECTLY TO THE CAMERA IT CREATES AN INSTINCTIVE SENSE THAT THE ANCHOR OR PUNDIT IS, YES, TALKING TO YOU WHILE YOU'RE WATCHING HIM/HER...

THIS IN TURN CREATES A SENSE FOR THE VIEWER THAT THEY KNOW THIS PERSON.

THAT YOU ARE SHARING AN INTIMATE RELATIONSHIP (A "PARASOCIAL" RELATIONSHIP) WITH HIM/HER...

S/HE FEELS LIKE A TRUSTED FRIEND, AND THUS WHATEVER NEWS OR INFORMATION S/HE GIVES YOU SEEMS MORE CREDIBLE...

I BELIEVE YOU!

WHAT THOSE STUDYING THE RELATIVELY NEW FIELD OF PARA-SOCIAL RELATIONSHIPS HAVE DEDUCED IS THAT THOUGH KIDS GROWING UP ON TV + FILMS EVENTUALLY COME TO UNDERSTAND THAT THE CHARACTERS THEY'RE "CONNECTING" WITH ON SCREEN ARE NOT REAL...

THAT EMOTIONAL CONNECTION THEY HAD WITH MR. ROGERS OR ELMO OR BART SIMPSON OR WONDER WOMAN WAS VERY REAL...

EVEN AT 35 YEARS OF AGE A PERSON WHO GREW UP WATCHING THE CHARACTERS OF THE ELABORATE HARRY POTTER UNIVERSE KNOW THAT THOSE CHARACTERS ARE NOT REAL...

... BUT STILL REMEMBERS THE FEELING OF BELIEVING THEY WERE...

THAT THE CHARACTERS WERE IN SOME WAYS TRUSTED FRIENDS THAT THEY KNEW...

HENCE WHEN WE SEE A CELEBRITY WE FEEL WE "KNOW" OR "TRUST" NAKED, IT CAN BE MORE ALLURING THAN A PERSON WE'RE NOT FAMILIAR WITH OR HAVE A PARASOCIAL RELATIONSHIP WITH...

1983 cult classic. Lattanzi's character's still in high school, Kaye's character's an older woman, they hook up, there's *tons* of sex and there's *tons* of great nudity.

I must have watched *My Tutor* at least fifty times. I love that film. If you grew up in the eighties or early nineties, you probably came across it. (And maybe across your television screen, too.)

Another gem from this period is *The Last American Virgin*. It might have one of the most depressing endings in the history of teenage sex comedies, but it didn't matter. Diane Franklin is naked in it two times. And she was *super* hot back then.

Everyone knows *Risky Business*. It's easy to think of this movie as "Tom Cruise's breakout film." But to me, the *real* breakout was Rebecca De Mornay and Cruise together in one of the greatest sex scenes of the 1980s.

Let me lob one at you that you probably haven't heard of before but that I would be remiss in my duties if I didn't suggest: *Mischief*. John Travolta's longtime wife Kelly Preston would later appear in such films as *The Cat in the Hat*, *For Love of the Game* and—coincidentally here—Tom Cruise-starrer *Jerry Maguire*. But when she was first getting started and twenty-one years old, it was the tail end of 1985 and no one knew who she was. Then there she was in *Mischief*: this beautiful blonde granting us some fantastic full-frontal. Well worth the watch, my friends!

TEEN SEX COMEDIES

Cheerleaders, virgins, panty raids, nerds, and naked pool parties—the rises and falls of Mr. Skin's favorite naked movie genre.

In March 1982, a low-budget, R-rated Canadian high school farce exploded in theaters like an atomic blast of pranks, peeping, partying, and all-points nudity and, on impact, immediately drew a naked line in movie history: *Porky's* proved to be the full-frontal flashpoint of the 1980s teen sex comedy revolution.

Prior to *Porky's*, of course, teens and sex and comedies had come together on screen, initially by way of the 1960s' nudity-free, but not-so-squeaky-clean Frankie-and-Annette beach party flicks.

Then, come the '70s, naked pep squad babes boosted more than spirits all over drive-ins in beloved raunch romps like *The Cheerleaders*, *The Pom-Pom Girls*, and *Cheerleaders' Wild Weekend*.

Even in the '80s, *Private Lessons* paved the way for *Porky's*. A major surprise hit about a high-school horndog who gets seduced by his sexy French teacher, *Private Lessons* effectively popped the box office cherry that allowed *Porky's* to subsequently gush so prolifically over the ensuing half-decade.

So as *Porky's* lit up Summer 1982, it was followed over the next few months by *The Last American Virgin*, *Zapped!*, *Losin' It*, *The Beach Girls*, and most spectacularly, *Fast Times at Ridgemont High*.

From there, the teen sex comedy onslaught seemed unstoppable. Every weekend, cinematic celebrations of pubescent lust packed multiplexes. Then the movies took on second and, in some cases, infinite lives via the era's definitive entertainment tech development: home video.

The standouts of this onslaught are classics by any standard: *Risky Business*, *My Tutor*, *Hardbodies*, *Valley Girl*, *Private School*, *Joysticks*, *Screwballs*, *Class*, *Revenge of the Nerds*, *Spring Break*, *Hot Dog...The Movie*, *Just One of the Guys*...the list goes on and on.

Alas, it didn't go on forever. It's impossible for anyone under forty to imagine now, but in 1983 when *Time* magazine decried "tits-and-zits" comedies overtaking the movies, it pinpointed the genre's most elemental appeal: these movies supplied the only reliable and even realistic way for adolescent males to actually see naked female breasts. (*National Lampoon*, the creators of *Animal House*, outright admit this was a major appeal of their entire comedy empire in both the recent documentary and feature film based on their history.)

Nudie mags couldn't be easily acquired. Hardcore porn films played in actual theaters that no sane teenager would want to enter even if he could. And anything resembling an "internet" remained at least a decade in the future.

As a result, to get a gander at bare gazongas, boys had to buy a ticket to the likes of *Mischief*, *Making the Grade*, or *Hamburger: The Motion Picture* and/or then record them off cable or rent them from the corner tape shop.

Still, the rage continued unabated until two crashers pooped the party: the PG-13 rating and John Hughes, a once-savage *National Lampoon* editor who inexplicably reinvented himself as cinema's sensitive teen-flick kingpin supreme.

First, the PG-13 allowed studios to appeal to a vastly larger audience than merely boner-brandishing bozos in high school. Nudity, in service of the new rating, shriveled up quick.

After the PG-13 rating came Hughes, who elevated his muse Molly Ringwald to universal teen queen status and upended the gender-based status quo. So, whereas *Porky's* and its progeny were all about guys getting off, the Hughes-Ringwald watersheds *Sixteen Candles*, *The Breakfast Club*, and *Pretty in Pink* were all about girls having actual feelings. And keeping their clothes on.

On top(less) of that, as video stores boomed, bona fide X-rated material became ever easier for young dudes to get their one-free-mitt on. In that context, how could even the mighty *Porky's* shower scene possibly compete with a VHS copy of *Hot Wet Anal Teen Screamers*?

American Pie briefly revived the teen sex comedy at the tail end of the twentieth century. But it was a flash in the pan(ts). The 1980s teen sex comedy is a thing of the past—but I've made it my business to keep it naked forever!

Don't get me wrong: I *did* have other interests back then, as I still do now. Actually, they're mostly the same. Sure, celebrity nudity has always been a big passion of mine, but I was also a regular American boy who loved the national pastime. I played a *lot* of baseball growing up and was almost as obsessed with it as I was with celebrity nudity.

History has always been a serious passion of mine, too. While I'm writing this, I'm gorging on this humongous biography of Ulysses S. Grant by Ron Chernow. Grant *never* got naked in a single movie! Not once! Yet I still love reading about him, his gargantuan impact on the course of the Civil War, and memorizing facts from all manner of history in general.

If I wasn't so busy being Mr. Skin, I'd probably be taking online courses in American history, listening to lectures nonstop. I love, love, *love* history. When I was younger, I would go down to my grandparents' basement, where they had all their old lamps and other antiques wrapped in newspaper, and I'd snatch off the pages to read what was going on in the 1950s or whenever they had first been published.

I was totally mesmerized. American history fascinated me as much then as it does now. Which has always overlapped with my passion for baseball. Baseball itself has such a rich history, with so much to absorb. I can combine my two passions of history and baseball into one easily: *baseball history!*

So maybe it's not so unthinkable that my sister Kristina didn't realize until much later that I had this preternatural interest in celebrity nudity while we were growing up under the same roof. Because, even though it may seem up until now that nudity was *all* I was into, there really was a lot of baseball and history, too.

"It wasn't like, 'Where's Jim? Oh, he's in the basement doing that thing again,'" Kristina says. "His friends were aware of what he was up to with the tapes, but I never knew."

I was just a regular teenage boy, in the eyes of my family. Would I become a baseball star? Maybe. But a guy who's famous for knowing every nude scene ever? That was something Kristina and the rest of my family never thought would be my future until it started happening years later.

And now, as my company's human resources director, it's Kristina's future, too!

Before I wrap this part up, I gotta tell you about *the* film of this profoundly foundational time in my life.

It's late summer 1982, I head on out to the movie theater, and I'm sitting down to watch *Fast Times at Ridgemont High*.

It's Cameron Crowe's first screenplay (boy, and he *directed Jerry Maguire*; talk about synchronicity here). Anyway, he's barely a kid himself. He wrote the movie based on his book that, at twenty-three or so, was kind of like a real-life Drew Barrymore *Never Been Kissed* experience he had in which he went undercover for *Rolling Stone* as a high school kid for a semester or so in order to write about what it was like to be a typical student in the early eighties.

It's Amy Heckerling's directorial debut. She would go on to make such movies as *Clueless* and the *Look Who's Talking* trilogy.

But none of this mattered to me at the time.

What mattered to me at the time (and now as I write this) is that at fifty-one minutes into *Fast Times*, the remarkably stunning Phoebe Cates lustily emerges from the sparkling azure swimming pool and, in sensational, silky, sensuous slow-mo—punctuated by the Cars' "Moving in Stereo"—she pops off her tiny red bikini top, and we had then and there what remains *the greatest nude scene in the history of movies!*

It was all part of a masturbatory fantasy in the filthy mind of a character played by the young Judge Reinhold. There he was onscreen, banging his gavel in the bathroom, dreaming about a half-naked wet and wild Cates.

Could you blame him? Case dismissed!

It's not only such an incredible scene, it's also incredibly *rare*. Cates is like the Sandy Koufax of celebrity nudity, with her short window of success. She was only in a handful of movies over the course of her brief career and was nude only three times. And like Mr. Koufax, she is in the Hall of Fame...the Mr. Skin Hall of Fame!

Cates in *Fast Times* was the celebrity nudity equivalent of knocking the skin off the ball: marvelous to behold, but practically once in a lifetime. Whenever I get asked in interviews, I *always* say the best nude scene of all time is Phoebe Cates in *Fast Times at Ridgemont High*.

As tough as it was to be in my preteens in the seventies, it was absolutely amazing to be in my late teens in the eighties. Once again, I turned out to be at the right age, at the right time.

There was no way I could have known that the aforementioned changes in pop culture and technology would collude so spectacularly to launching me off on my way to becoming Mr. Skin.

PARADISE

Phoebe Cates popping open her red bikini top in *Fast Times at Ridgemont High* is my favorite celebrity nude scene of all time—it is the naked Hollywood moment toward which all previous naked Hollywood moments had led, and from which all subsequent naked Hollywood moments have proceeded.

That stated, believe it or not, another Phoebe Cates movie exists from the very same era that contains even more of her naked body, displayed more frequently, and in more blatantly sexual situations.

No, it's not *Private School*. Phoebe just barely flashes butt-crack in that teen sex raunch comedy favorite which does, by the way, feature Betsy Russell in the Greatest Topless on Horseback Scene of all time.

In fact, the actual winner when it comes to the most Phoebe Cates nudity in a single motion picture is *Paradise*. It's a blatant rip-off of the Brooke Shields smash *The Blue Lagoon*, shot in Israel and co-starring Willie Aames of TV's *Eight Is Enough* and *Charles in Charge* (and, later that year, the telekinetic T&A high school farce *Zapped!*).

In *Paradise*, Phoebe plays an American youngster traveling through the Middle East in 1823 when her caravan gets raided by an evil sheik on the hunt for teenage brides. She and Willie, who plays the son of American missionaries, escape to a tropical oasis and let puberty take its due course.

From there, Phoebe gets naked in six separate scenes, baring her boobs, butt, and even a glimpse at her lush lap-oasis. The movie's called *Paradise* for the breast of all possible reasons!

College!

It's funny how being a teenager who's obsessed with baseball or being a history nerd is considered perfectly normal, but you tell someone you've got the same knack for celebrity nudity and suddenly you're some kind of freak.

Thankfully, it wasn't really a problem for me. Kristina remembers how popular I was in my teens. Some of it was because of my playing baseball. Not surprisingly, though, a lot of my popularity in the teen community of my area stemmed from my boxes and boxes of celebrity nudity tapes.

This popularity lasted right into college.

Friends would come over to my dorm, we'd pop in a five-hour nudie scene highlights tape, down a few beers, and then go out for a night on the town. It was the perfect pregame!

My life was turning into a raunchy, goofy 1980s comedy. I was at Indiana University, not too far from where I'd grown up in suburban Chicago. It was here that I took an opportunity that a guy like me could not pass up. It was in truth an opportunity *no* guy could pass up.

I became a server at one of the best sororities on campus. You could have written it as a feature-length screenplay: *The Houseboy*, starring Jim McBride, a Mr. Skin Joint. Imagine: I'm twenty years old, a junior in college...and I'm waiting on all these insanely gorgeous young sorority girls.

They didn't even have to pay me. Sure, I got all the free meals I wanted, which was nice. But the *real* compensation came in the form of getting to be around all these delectable ladies.

There were two things I remember specifically from this real-life teen sex comedy-esque experience.

One was that I would be standing there with the other servers in our white coats, looking all prim and proper and respectable for our girls. We would be standing up straight against the walls of the dining room for 5:30 p.m. dinner, and all the girls would be waiting outside.

The doors would open, and in flocked the girls led by the house mom. There might be sixty or seventy of these beautiful college knockouts, each beaming with overpowering sexual energy and scented by intoxicating perfume. Drop-dead gorgeous, I'm telling you. A feast for the senses.

The second thing I recall specifically was the *coup de grâce*. Dinner was delicious, but breakfast? Epicurean. Sunday brunch was my bonus. If you worked Sunday mornings—which I would always try to do— you'd have the food ready for the girls in the kitchen, and in they'd come pitter-pattering on bare feet, in diaphanous nightgowns, silky pajamas, and see-through tank tops. They'd come bursting in without worry that we blushing servers were standing there red as beets.

The obvious question is, did I get to date any of these girls? *Come on*. What kind of a cad do you take me for? *Of course* I did! I was prime real estate for escorting them to different dinners and get-togethers, parties, and other events on their packed agendas. It was all about good times, especially if you have any comprehension of what girls in Indiana were like in the 1980s.

It was the highlight of my college career.

Let me explain something: I played baseball (center fielder) all through high school at Oak Park River Forest (*go Huskies!*) before graduating in 1981. We won the state championship of Illinois my senior year, and I got a full ride to play ball at St. Xavier College in Chicago. I only stayed one year, though, and quit because I got burned out from playing eighty-six games that spring. I transferred to Indiana University, where I decided not to play.

SIDE-BUSH: PROFILES IN FURRAGE

At MrSkin.com, we're forever coming across eye-popping patterns of nakedness and trying to come up with side-splitting nicknames for them—e.g., "Marty Feldman Boobs" for nipples that point in different directions like the eyes of the vintage funnyman; or a "Larry Fine" for when a lady's lap-curls protrude from the sides of her panties in the manner of the wild-maned Stooge (in the case of black actresses, we call that an "Oscar Gamble").

When it comes to muffs so fluffy they visibly protrude even when not facing front, there's just no beating the term "side-bush."

As a proponent of powerfully full-grown pubes, the side-bush is one of my absolute favorite ways to see an actress bare by way of her hair-down-there. Here are some of my favorite examples:

- **Jill Clayburgh**—*La Luna* (1:05) Director Bernardo Bertolucci's obscure incest drama stars Jill as a mom who loves her son deeply and, when she turns sideways bottomless, lushly and thickly, too.
- **Leslie Bega**—*Time of Her Time* (1:28) After leaping from bed to pull on her clothes, Leslie delivers an askew view of her short-hairs grown long.
- **Kathleen Beller**—*The Betsy* (0:13) Best known for playing Kirby on the '80s TV sensation *Dynasty* and, in real life, long married to '80s one-hit wonder Thomas Dolby ("She Blinded Me With Science"), Kathleen scorched the '70s by showing side-rug during her *Betsy*-opening skinny-dip.

It's one of the only regrets of my entire life that I didn't stay at St. Xavier and keep playing ball. I *totally* should have kept at it for all four years of college. I played some semipro in my twenties and loved it, but I wasn't as in shape as I could have been if I had been playing in college.

This is something I still think about every now and then, but you know what? I got to be the houseboy at that Indiana U sorority, so hey, that's not such a bad consolation prize!

Really: think of what it was like for this guy who had been growing up on *Porky's* and *Animal House* and was now *living* that life.

You can imagine what a thrill this college debauchery was for a young Mr. Skin-to-be. I was already compiling my own Skinfinition lexicon when I got to see my very first "Larry Fine" (also known as an "Oscar Gamble," it's what occurs when a girl's bush sticks out of either side of her lacy underwear; for the uninitiated, look up either "Larry Fine" or "Oscar Gamble" and you'll immediately see what I mean).

Even with all of this going on all around me in my real day-to-day life, I never gave up on continuing to grow my collection of tapes. I even became more sophisticated in how I organized my archive.

What I would do was take a sheet of paper and write up a log of every box, every tape, every scene on each five-hour compilation. I would indulge in incredible detail: who was nude, how far into the movie she was nude, which body parts were exposed. I ended up with these long-ass sheets of paper that I would then fold up and slip into each videotape box.

I'm fairly certain that when I die, the Smithsonian will want to get their hands on my personal collection of celebrity nudity tapes and archival notes. I really was that meticulous. It was the same kind of fixation that people have long had when it comes to collecting baseball cards, comic books, stamps, and action figures. *I had to have it all!* And it all needed to be complete and accurate in full detail.

You've heard of a Rhodes Scholar? Well, back then, my friends would joke I was a *Loads* Scholar. I'd like to think I remain one to this day!

FIVE SKINTASTIC NUDE SCENES THAT FLEW UNDER THE RADAR

When A-list superstars have dared to go amazingly bare—and, somehow, only Mr. Skin seemed to notice!

5. **Mimi Rogers**—*The Door in the Floor* (0:46)
4. **Salma Hayek**—*Ask the Dust* (0:33)
3. **Jessica Biel**—*Powder Blue* (1:08)
2. **Anne Hathaway**—*Havoc* (0:36)
1. **Rosario Dawson**—*Trance* (1:01)

Work at the Merc

A few years out of college, I realized the inevitable: it was time to move out of my parents' basement.

In 1992, I got a job at the Chicago Mercantile Exchange. I started as a runner and worked my way up to the vaunted role of "clerk." Ho-boy!

I was really moving on up to the east side and finally getting a piece of the pie. Just not the right kind.

The job had me watching desks as phone clerks would flash orders to me, and then I'd relay the orders to the brokers in the Eurodollar pit. When there was a fast market, the place would erupt into maddening pandemonium. You've never seen such chaos, except maybe in the TV shows and movies about Wall Street that show *only* how savage it can get. Everyone scrambling around, slamming into one another and holding up their bid cards, yelling and moving vampirically fast for hours on end.

Then there were the times that you *don't* see in the movies and on TV. *Slow* times. *Really* slow. Boring slow. It's these times at the Merc that I remember as the best times. Since nothing was being traded on the floor, we'd end up sitting around like a bunch of tired athletes in the locker room.

That's me in the Eurodollar pit at the Chicago Mercantile Exchange—somewhere! I worked as a clerk at the Merc, and in between global mega-deals, I doled out information to the titans of finance about what actresses got nude in which movies.

"WHAT A RUNNER/CLERK DOES"

YOU PROBABLY HAVEN'T EVER WONDERED WHAT A "RUNNER" OR "CLERK" DOES ON THE STOCK MARKET FLOOR...

BUT, THAT'S WHAT MR. SKIN DID BEFORE HE WAS MR. SKIN

"THE PIT" IS THE AREA OF THE TRADING FLOOR WHERE PEOPLE ARE BUYING AND SELLING VARIOUS KINDS OF "SECURITIES" OR STOCKS...

...THROUGH A SYSTEM IN WHICH THEY'RE ALL LITERALLY SHOUTING BACK AND FORTH "BUY" OR "SELL" ORDERS LIKE YOU'VE SEEN IN MOVIES OR ON T.V....

THESE PEOPLE ARE MOSTLY "BROKERS". THE BROKERS CAN ALSO BE BACK AT THEIR DESKS ON THE PHONE WITH INVESTORS TELLING THEM WHAT TO BUY AND SELL...

NOW, THE NEXT PLAYER HERE IS AN "ARB CLERK"... OR AS MR.SKIN USED TO CALL IT AN "AB" CLERK

A KIND OF LIASON BETWEEN THE BROKERS OR CLERKS AT THEIR DESKS TALKING TO INVESTORS BY PHONE AND THE ACTION GOING ON IN THE PIT.

THE LAST PLAYER WORTH MENTIONING HERE IS THE "RUNNER"...

A RUNNER IS TYPICALLY A NEW HIRE ON THE FLOOR, OR A YOUNG COLLEGE/HS KID DOING A SUMMER JOB...

THINK OF THEM LIKE THE ASSISTANTS OR GOFERS FOR THE OTHER PLAYERS IN THE PIT...

...OR AT THE DESKS HELPING TO MAKE SURE EVERYTHING IS MOVING SMOOTHLY...

OR AS SMOOTHLY AS CAN BE IMAGINED, CONSIDERING THE WHOLE THING IS TOTAL SWEATY STRESS AND CHAOS...

EXCEPT WHEN IT'S A SLOW MARKET AND PEOPLE ARE JUST STANDING AROUND...

...HOPING TO BE ENTERTAINED BY A BURGEONING MR. SKIN...

WHO IS HIMSELF DREAMING OF MAKING HIS WAY OUT AND DOING SOMETHING ELSE ENTIRELY.

LUCKILY FOR SKIN, HE DID JUST THAT...

MERC

AND NOW YOU'RE READING HIS BOOK!

MR SKIN BOOK

I may not have been the best clerk in a fast market. But during the slow hours, I shined. Why? It was when we were in the doldrums marketwise that the brokers at the Merc began discovering there was this weird guy who, if you were to ask him about any actress—any actress at all—he'd tell you off the top of his head if she'd been naked in a film and how far into the movie you'd have to go to find the scene.

I'd be standing there with my pals with nothing to do. We're talking *crickets*. Nothing going on in the pit. Dead snakes, all of us. Clock-watching. *Yawn.*

Then some runner girl would shove a note in my hand. Her phone number, maybe? No. A test, given to her by one of the traders in the pits. The TV show *Mad About You* had been pretty big at the time (early nineties) and starred Paul Reiser and Helen Hunt.

The note read: "Has Helen Hunt ever done a nude scene?" I sent a note back replying, "Oh, yeah. Of course. She did a movie called *The Waterdance* with Eric Stoltz. She shows breast and butt at the 0:51 minute mark."

But there was something else that would happen in these situations that continued to form me into Mr. Skin. It wasn't enough that I knew all the celeb nude scenes in the world. It wasn't enough that I could tell you everything you wanted to know about them and the actresses featured.

When I'd messenger my reply back to the brokers, I'd instinctively include a joke. In the case of Helen Hunt, I might have written something like, "...and she'll probably give you a Reiser when you see it!"

The chain reaction was catalytic. This young runner girl would be all quiet and calm, bored like the rest of us. She'd walk my note all serious back to the middle of the pit to the guys in there, and then suddenly they'd erupt into a bedlam of resounding laughter.

It helped us pass the time when things got too quiet.

A broker might ask about Ashley Judd, another popular lady during the nineties. "Sure!" I'd write. "Check out *Normal Life* or *Norma Jean and Marilyn*. Two of my *favorite* movies to see her naked in!"

How about the one and only Demi Moore? *Very* popular back then. Also, *very* well known as someone who often got naked. So, the guys would ask me, "What's the *best* movie to see her naked in?"

Easy answer: *Striptease*. There she is, with our old buddy Burt Reynolds again, an hour and seventeen minutes in, and she's dirty dancing for him. I'd tell the brokers they *had* to check out the movie, and would make sure to include that they could see way "moore" of Demi than they could have ever hoped.

Being the nineties, another beloved TV series was *Friends*. Everyone was gaga over the girls on that show. Nobody at the Merc could believe that I knew about a super-obscure movie called *Blue Desert*. Why would I know about the film? Because of a young actress it featured who would later go on to fame and fortune in *Friends*: Courteney Cox.

In *Blue Desert*, about an hour and fourteen minutes in, Cox is naked in bed. Me being me, wanting to be as detailed and accurate as possible, I made sure to note in my reply that you could see her breasts...but that when she got out of the bed in the nude, they were using a body double.

As with our tongue-in-cheek comedy stylings on MrSkin.com, this compulsion to be extremely detailed and accurate is something that remains a core principle on the website. We can get *insanely* detailed, in fact, at Mr. Skin. With good reason: people know when they visit us online that they won't see fake pics or false information. No #fakenews at Mr. Skin! But, we'll get to that later, too.

FIVE MOST SKINFAMOUS BODY DOUBLES

When the stars shied away from showing flesh, these heroic substitutes stripped down for them.

5. **Vida Guerra for Ana de la Reguera**—*Eastbound & Down* (S2, E3)
4. **Shelley Michelle for Julia Roberts**—*Pretty Woman* (movie poster)
3. **Michelle Derstine for Melissa Rauch**—*The Bronze* (1:20)
2. **Catherine Bell for Isabella Rossellini**—*Death Becomes Her* (1:19)
1. **Victoria Lynn Johnson for Angie Dickinson**—*Dressed to Kill* (0:02)

Skinfining Moment #1: Skin on Tap

So, working at the Chicago Mercantile Exchange turned out to be a good gig for me, even during the many dead times. *Especially* during those boring periods, because this was when—over those four or five years of being a runner and clerk—I was honing my craft. My craft as an informer and, more importantly, my craft as an entertainer.

It wasn't about financial rewards. There weren't any for this ridiculous parlor trick of mine. It was just something I did, because I was bored, a little nutty, and happened to have this ludicrous amount of data crammed in my head.

Right around this time, I had my first Skinfining Moment.

I'm in Chicago's Lincoln Park area, at a bar called Charlie's Ale House in the fall of 1996. I'm not sure if anyone remembers the bar, but it doesn't matter. What *does* matter is that this was where I would go all the time with my friends after work. Practically every weeknight, I'd be there.

It didn't make a difference to me that I had to be up early the following mornings. (I would have to be on the floor of the Merc at 7:00 a.m. *sharp*.) But I'm nevertheless getting blissfully soused at Charlie's Ale House on a Tuesday night. 11:00 p.m. As I'm knocking back beer after beer, my pals inevitably begin quizzing me about actresses.

I'm answering each question without fail. I'm on my typical roll. No one can stump me. I check my watch: *Damn! I gotta get home! It's getting late!*

Right as I'm about to announce, "Well, guys, that's it: time for bed," someone taps me on the shoulder. His name was Harry Teinowitz. Still is, in fact. Harry had just started broadcasting a midday Chicago radio show. I didn't know him before this encounter, but he's since become one of my dearest friends.

Harry tells me about his radio show and that he's been eavesdropping on my rattling off all this celebrity nudity trivia. "You've been blowing my mind all night!" he says. "Would you be willing to come on my radio show and have people call in to ask you questions?"

That's me in 1999 alongside Harry Teinowitz. The long road to the Skinpire began two years earlier when Harry overheard me rattling off nudity stats in a bar and asked me to guest on his show. Since I was then skittish about using my real name, Harry dubbed me "Mr. Skin." The rest is Skinstory!

Bleary-eyed and a little wobbly, I looked right at Harry and said, "I'll do it, but I don't want to use my real name. My parents have no idea what a freak I am. I don't want to go on as 'Jim McBride.'"

"No problem, dude," Harry says. "Let's come up with a moniker."

I said that was a good idea, and Harry comes back with, "How about 'Mr. Naked'?"

"Harry," I say, "that's really creepy."

That's when he says it. And I swear, this is a true story. It only took two tries for Harry to blurt out, "How about...'Mr. Skin'?"

I say that'll work, and that I'll be on his radio show.

A few days later, I'm in a cab on my way from the Merc to Harry's studio at the Hancock Building. It's my lunch break.

I am *nervous!* This would be my first-ever appearance on a radio show. I had never even called in to a show before. But I was a fan of local radio and have to say that my anxiety added something to my performance. It got me fired up.

Harry couldn't have been nicer to me when I was on his show. He was so cool. He talked me up, tossed some easy softball questions to help me get the ball rolling, and then opened the phone lines.

POW: I'm on there for twenty minutes, I'm taking calls and cracking every ball right out of the park. It was *fun!*

People have likened me to Rain Man with this wacky talent for memorizing celebrity nudity trivia, but I'm not like the plain, almost robotic Dustin Hoffman character in the eponymous film.

Though I'm fine with people referencing the Rain Man character in describing what it is I do as Mr. Skin, the sense of humor I have about it all and that we employ throughout the website is a crucial component of the brand.

That first time on radio, on Harry's show, sealed the deal in my mind: I *had* to be funny about celebrity nudity to make this whole thing work. Again, I didn't want to just inform, I wanted to entertain.

I don't know where these jokes come from; I guess from the same place where I store all the celebrity nudity information itself. Somewhere deep in my wacky brain.

Wherever it comes from, there I was, on Harry's show, and someone called in to ask if Julie *"Mary Poppins/Sound of Music"* Andrews had ever been naked in a film.

"Oh, yeah," I answered. "She did a Blake Edwards movie in 1981 called *S.O.B.*, and at the hour-and-forty-five-minute mark…*her hills were alive!*"

My schtick as Mr. Skin had officially gone public.

FIVE ACTRESSES YOU WON'T BELIEVE DID A NUDE SCENE

You know them. You don't think of them as the type to flash flesh. Here's when to see them naked.

5. **Julie Andrews**—*S.O.B.* (1:20)

4. **Ellen DeGeneres**—*If These Walls Could Talk 2* (0:15)

3. **Vanna White**—*Gypsy Angels* (1:04)

2. **Molly Ringwald**—*Malicious* (0:40)

1. **Maureen McCormick**—*Texas Lightning* (1:19)

Everyone in the studio began laughing. *Hard*. We were having a blast throughout the entire twenty minutes I was on the air. As I was watching everyone in the studio laughing and smiling, it hit me like a ton of bricks: *this is the greatest thing in the world.*

I loved being on the radio. I loved being Mr. Skin.

I knew, though, that my fifteen minutes of fame were nearly expired. Soon, I'd be heading back to the Chicago Mercantile Exchange, my lunch break would be over, and I'd be languishing at a job that was becoming less and less appealing to me.

For the rest of that day, I couldn't stop thinking about being Mr. Skin. I couldn't stop thinking about how, as I had been leaving Harry's studio, I'd gotten another life-changing tap on my shoulder. This time from Harry's producer, Wonder Boy.

"My god," he said breathlessly, "we had so many people who wanted to talk with you. Would you be willing to come back on some time?"

The moment with Harry's producer flashed in my mind over and over again as I worked the rest of the day at the Merc, headed out to Charlie's Ale House to hang with my friends, and watched as everyone kept cracking up at how much I knew about celebrity nudity.

"Man, I really have something here," I remember thinking. "But what?"

What's a Website?

Pretty soon, I'm a regular on Harry's radio show. I'm killing it. More importantly, it continued to teach me how to *keep* killing it on radio… and how to be Mr. Skin.

Harry would have me on once a month. Which meant people all over Chicago were discovering Mr. Skin and this truly bizarre talent he had. It was no longer just my buddies in high school, classmates in college, the barflies at Charlie's Ale House, or colleagues at the Merc who knew about what I could do.

I would take another leap forward when a much bigger Chicago radio program—*The Steve Dahl Show*—chicken-hawked me from Harry and started having me on over *there*. So now an even larger swath of Chicago's populace was hearing Mr. Skin miraculously nail question after question about celebrity nudity.

BUDDING SKINSPIRATIONS

The celebrity nudity resources that launched my life's work—loin-first.

Back when I was *coming*-of-age as a celebrity nudity *buff* (every possible pun intended there), spotting naked moments in movies meant having to keep a constant eye (and one free hand) on what was new in theaters, on cable TV, down at the video rental store—and then watching all of it.

Fortunately, even in that exhausting pre-digital era, a small band of pioneers blazed the way for devotees like me to find out about—and even openly ogle—breaking nudes and the entire history of Hollywood hotties in the raw.

As a result, Mr. Skin became possible because I was standing on the laps of these giants:

- *Playboy*'s "Sex in Cinema." Since 1965, *Playboy* magazine's annual "Sex in Cinema" feature has highlighted the best and barest big-screen moments of the previous twelve months, complete with still photos of stunningly naked movie starlets. It stuffs more than my stocking every year.

- *Celebrity Skin* magazine. Founded in 1976 by an absolute genius who deems himself "Celebrity Sleuth," *Celebrity Skin*, which started as a one-issue spin-off of *High Society* magazine, sold out at news-stands in a skinstant and quickly became its own monthly title that ran for decades. The Sleuth, who worked for the original parent company that put out *Celebrity Skin*, simply could not be contained, though, and, in due time, rewrote the famous T&A nude-iverse by breaking out on his own.

- *Celebrity Sleuth* magazine. Ten years after he established what had been the definitive Tinseltown T&A publication, Celebrity Sleuth busted out with a magazine named after himself that, more than anything else, directly effected (and erected) the phenomenon that would become Mr. Skin. From rare pics of the highest quality to authoritative research written in uproariously pun-tastic style, I will forever salute Celebrity Sleuth as the origin of my species!

- *The Bare Facts Video Guide* by Craig Hosoda. Bypassing photographs, but piling on obsessive information about the unblinking details of movie nude scenes, *The Bare Facts Video Guide* laid bare how important it was to list titles, actresses' names, down-to-the-minute times, and exactly who shows which parts of her body.

One of Dahl's producers was friends with a guy who worked on a show in Boston called *Matty in the Morning*. So, I started going on *Matty* in Boston. Whose tenure led to my becoming friendly with a producer at *that* program who hooked me up with Seattle's *The Bob Rivers Show*. Which meant Mr. Skin was now broadcasting coast-to-coast.

It's the mid-nineties. Mr. Skin is being heard all over the country, and I have nothing to promote. Nothing to *sell*. Nothing to drive listeners and my growing fan base toward in order to turn what I was doing into something more than a nationwide bar trick.

I'm a pretty simple guy, so part of me was fine with the fact that I wasn't making a killing while I killed it on radio shows around the country. It was just a whole lot of fun talking about celebrity nudity all the time to people in all these major cities.

Meanwhile, I had to keep going to my *real* job at the Merc. And my bosses were starting to become less cool with me constantly heading out to be Mr. Skin on the radio.

"Come on, man," they'd complain. "You're leaving work all the time, doing all these shows. *We're not paying you for that.*"

You know something? They were 100 percent right.

I wasn't being paid by my bosses to become a radio celebrity. I was being paid to do something that was in fact inhibiting my growth as Mr. Skin. I needed to figure this out.

Summer, 1998.

I'm umping a celebrity softball game. They're broadcasting the game live on Chicago's WCKG, which has a huge listenership.

The game's over, I'm tying my shoe, and it's already late; it had been a night game. I'm thinking about how I gotta get home and get to sleep, because—*man!*—I gotta be up and at 'em at the Merc the next morning.

That's when this guy comes up to me. Yup: basically another tap on the shoulder. The guy says that he listens to me all the time on *The Steve Dahl Show*.

"Dude, you're great," he continues. "Would you ever consider doing a website?"

Don't forget: it's 1998. So, it shouldn't be too surprising that my initial knee-jerk response was, "What the heck's a website?"

I mean, especially for those super-nerds out there, you know that the net had only just become fully commercialized three years earlier. Amazon.com had only launched four years before this. It was six years before Facebook. It was a few months before *Google* launched, for goodness' sake.

The normal person on the street did not know what a website was, or at least didn't care. Not that I was ever normal. But, yeah: *What's a website?*

The guy explains that a website is something that can make me *money*. Ahhh...*that's* a website.

"My company can help you build one," the digital huckster pitches me. "If you can raise some money, we can make it happen."

I'm intrigued. Here I am, not only Mr. Skin, but once again Mr. Lucky. Right time, right place, right now. And I'm getting excited.

But first I needed to understand more about this whole "online" thing. I found some kid at the Merc (I myself was around thirty-five at the time) who had a computer hooked up to the internet at his apartment.

He's happy to show it off to me, and we're talking *dial-up* here. The kid's using Yahoo! Search.

I ask him to show me some celebrity nudity.

I can't remember exactly what he showed me, but I *can* remember my reaction: "That *sucks!*"

We kept exploring, and not only did everything look horrendous, it wasn't organized or the least bit informative. You'd find Angelina Jolie naked, but there'd be no context detailing where the pic was from or how far into the movie you could find it yourself. No jokes. No pizzazz. No *nothin'!*

I can do better than that!

Who knows why I thought this was true: I had been online for only a few minutes, but already I knew I *could* do better. Way better.

Erecting Mr. Skin

Right off, I had a checklist popping up in my head of ten things I could do to improve on what was already out there when it came to celebrity nudity compilations.

Knowing I had a special concept, I went out and raised seventy thousand dollars. Some came from my brother-in-law and some came from a broker I knew at the Merc who had confidence in me after seeing what I could do as Mr. Skin.

With the money in hand, I was able to hire the web developer who had originally come up to me and said, "Wanna make a website?"

Now I was trying to get my website off the ground *and* laboring away at the Merc full-time. It was grueling. It became impossible. Something had to give. I had to make a difficult decision. Or, maybe now that I look back on it, it wasn't so difficult after all.

Whatever the case, I realized quickly that I had to go all in with MrSkin.com. I quit my job at the Merc on March 5, 1999, and my website and company became my full-time gig. Which means now I had to be Mr. Skin full-time, too.

TOP TEN NUDE SCENES OF 1999

The best of the breast (and beyond) from the very year MrSkin.com launched.

10. **Ali Larter**—*Varsity Blues* (0:52)
 9. **Hilary Swank**—*Boys Don't Cry* (1:22)
 8. **Tara Reid**—*Body Shots* (1:07)
 7. **Kate Winslet**—*Holy Smoke!* (1:04)
 6. **Nicollette Sheridan**—*Raw Nerve* (0:24)
 5. **Kelly Monaco**—*Idle Hands* (1:07)
 4. **Mena Suvari**—*American Beauty* (1:46)
 3. **Rene Russo**—*The Thomas Crown Affair* (1:13)
 2. **Nicole Kidman**—*Eyes Wide Shut* (0:21)
 1. **Shannon Elizabeth**—*American Pie* (0:44)

The bleak reality was that I was already thirty-six, nearly thirty-seven years old, living paycheck to paycheck while I had been at the Merc. It's not as though I was leaving behind some lucrative two-hundred-thousand-dollar-a-year dream job. This was a significant factor in not really caring that I was leaving the Merc behind to hop full throttle into being Mr. Skin.

I've had friends over the course of my life who *were* making six figures earlier on, and because of that fact, if an opportunity came along for them to do something else, they wouldn't take the risk. Knowing myself, if *I* had been making that kind of money at the Merc or anywhere else, I probably wouldn't have left it behind to become self-employed. I would have been too scared to lose what I had.

It was my *lack* of success, then, that was the deciding factor in my choosing to pursue something that would ultimately lead to my success further down the road.

In those first few days and weeks, though, it was just Mr. Skin and me. I had to make it work. This would be how I would pay my bills. I was employing people like my web developer. Meanwhile, I had to write *all* the content for the site.

I had to put together all the actress bios, all the reviews, oversee all the handling of stills and clips. This meant eighteen-hour days in my miniature, cramped studio apartment.

And I loved every minute of it.

This was exactly what I wanted to be doing with my life. With pressure mounting, me hemorrhaging money, and without being able to do anything except work on the website, I was having a blast.

It was the first job I was ever really good at, and my faith in what I was doing never once waned. Even if I was totally exhausted, practically broke, and spending almost every waking minute at the computer.

I knew I needed some help, so I brought in a friend or two, and my sister Kristina, to assist me. She always laughs when she brings up the day I called and told her to watch the local news for a segment they aired in which they revealed that *I* was this Mr. Skin character who had been making the rounds on the local radio scene.

"I was like, 'What the hell? This is so bizarre!'" Kristina recalls. "Then he tells me he quit his job and goes, 'Oh, by the way…would you want to help do data entry? *For my new company?*' It was crazy."

I was finally indulging fully in my lifelong obsession, and it was everything I had hoped it would be. If you were to ask any of my friends or family, they would tell you that I was spending *all* my waking hours on building the site. For at least six months straight, almost never leaving my pocket-size hobbit hole apartment.

My wife Michelle remembers my self-imposed spartan routine. We had just started dating, and sometimes she'd be staying over, trying to sleep while I would be up until 3:00 a.m. at the glowing computer screen, boomingly clacking away on my loud-ass keyboard.

Poor Michelle was a young lawyer on the rise and would have to be at the courthouse at 9:00 a.m. She'd be attempting to sleep with the pillow pulled around her face. She'd finally fall asleep, before the alarm would go off at six in the morning…and I'd just be getting up too, to *also* get back to work, whether it was calling in for my radio spots or adding to my website.

"I remember saying to him, 'Hey, *I'm* the attorney! *I'm* the one who's supposed to be working crazy hours!'" laughs Michelle as she recalls our hungrier days together.

"We actually broke up at one point because of how much he was working," she added. "We got back together, obviously, but I couldn't believe it: I was working seven days a week at this goddamn law firm, and Jim was working even crazier hours than I was! He was working more hours than a young lawyer or young doctors. That's how hard he was working to launch Mr. Skin."

Michelle recalls too that I was "so dedicated to *every fucking detail!* If somebody else had been doing it, they wouldn't have cared about whether or not there was some small nip slip in a certain scene in a specific movie or not. Jim isn't like that. For him, it has to *all* be right."

There was no question in my mind that I required detailed Skinformation on *one thousand* actresses before I could launch MrSkin.com. Why one thousand? I didn't want someone to come to my site, search around for fifteen minutes, say, "Well, I guess I've seen all there is to see," and move on. I wanted those people to stick around.

I had been given seventy thousand dollars to make sure MrSkin.com not only worked but would be a viral success. I wasn't going to let down myself or any of the other people in my life who believed in me.

Kristina's memory of those days involves her coming over after finishing up at her day job, entering my apartment carpeted with VHS tapes and DVDs, and me tapping her in to enter information into my ever-growing database.

Her help allowed me to go out to at least get a bite to eat or work out at the gym. I could use these brief stints to rest my eyes for a few hours here or there. It was nice having someone to fix my typos, help me broaden my archive, and let me get away from the computer once in a rare while.

There were times when people—even Kristina—had their doubts. Would anyone actually pay to be a subscriber to our site? Would studio and network lawyers come banging on our door? Would the whole thing completely come tumbling down upon launching?

"When he first told us he was going to quit his job and develop a website, we were like, 'What? What do you mean?'" remembers one of my closest, longtime friends, Pete.

Pete eventually came onboard full-time to be my radio booking guy, but back in 1999, he recalls my "sitting in [Jim's] apartment for months where we wouldn't see Jim at all. He'd be compiling all this information in his database, and we all finally said, 'Okay...,' assuming the whole thing would last, maybe, six months. Then he'd go back to work at the Merc."

Nips ahoy! Cruising Lake Michigan in 1999 with radio host Pete McMurray during a live broadcast on WCKG. Pete made me a regular weekly guest on his show for years, and he's been a huge part of the Skinpire since then.

I knew better. I knew it would work. I was so optimistic with what we were doing and how we were doing it. I knew so deeply that other people would be as into it as I was. Enough so that, yes, they would *pay* for it. I knew we would be fine.

I'm so grateful that people like Kristina and other supporters were there for me. They could see it in my eyes that I had something worthwhile going on here. And they wanted to come along with me for the wild ride ahead.

It's why Michelle encouraged and stood by me. Sure, she thought the whole thing was silly and funny, but she also believed in me. She was there to watch me put the site together and saw how into it I was, how well I was doing on all these radio show appearances.

She'll tell you no one could ever accuse her of being a gold digger, and it's true: Michelle was there with me when I had *nothing* except for a radical concept and an unsinkable drive.

In the very beginning, in my studio apartment days, I had *no* money. *Everything* was going into the business, and the business wasn't reciprocating. I had raised just enough money to get set for launching and to barely—*barely*—pay my own living expenses. I may have paid myself a salary of fifteen thousand dollars.

For our first date, I took Michelle to this restaurant called Rosebud. I chose Rosebud because I had gift certificates from all the times I would go on a radio show that Pete was producing at the time. Even though Pete's show, *Radio for Men*, was sponsored by *Playboy*, he still had no money either. So, he'd give his guests gift certificates, and I'd turn around and use them so I could eat. Or, in this case, take my wife-to-be Michelle out on a date.

For our second date, I invited Michelle over for a nice home-cooked meal. By "home cooked," I mean microwaved. Leftovers. From Rosebud. (Where else?) But, boy was I a pro by this point at heating up leftovers. The late, great Anthony Bourdain would have been proud. And so was Michelle.

"I knew the site was going to be good," she says.

The two of us were sitting by a lake one beautiful sunset-lit evening, and Michelle turned to me suddenly to proclaim just how proud of me she was.

I had my in: "Are you proud enough to be my wife?"

On August 10, 1999, at 4:45 p.m. CST, with one thousand actresses and four hundred movie clips, we flipped the switch.

It may be hard for some of my younger readers in particular to grasp this, but launching a website in the summer of 1999 was a matter of steering right into the unknown. There wouldn't even be such a thing as Wikipedia for nearly two years. It was the Wild West days of the internet as a public and commercial utility. Anything could happen.

Luckily, anything did.

By 4:50 p.m.—literally five minutes after launch—I got my first "join" (subscriber). Wow! Someone was paying to be a member of my website. Some guy from Cincinnati who shelled out a whopping $4.95 for a three-day pass to MrSkin.com. I remember thinking, "Man, this is going to be easy!"

Right.

Six months passed, and we were still touch and go. Yeah, we were getting joins, but I wasn't making enough money. Michelle remembers that I was sustaining myself on maybe two or three hours of sleep a night. It was such a slog that we celebrated my seventieth join.

Yes, we celebrated getting *seventy* memberships. Seven. Zero.

Skinfining Moment #2: Howard Gets Skinned

I was getting a harsh lesson in the reality of the new business of online commerce. Which was when Skinfining Moment #2 happened, right when I needed it most.

It was probably the best thing that ever happened in my professional life. I still remember the exact minute: it was at 8:20 a.m. on March 23, 2000, that I was asked to be on Howard Stern's radio show and happily accepted the lifesaving invitation.

Friends had been pushing me to go on the show for months, but I hadn't felt ready. This might be another reason why I've been able to survive all these years: Someone else might have pounced on the chance to be on *Howard Stern* way too soon. Especially back when Howard was the *king* of radio, when his show was syndicated *everywhere*, and

Birth of a birthday suit business. Here's the front page of MrSkin.com on August 10, 1999 at 4:45 p.m.—the moment the site went live. As proven by that free clip art image of cartoon cop, aesthetic excellence was a *top* priority from the very beginning.

when it meant that *everyone in the entire country* would hear you if you were blessed with the opportunity to be on his show.

People thought I was crazy to hesitate the way I did.

"You'll make so much money!" they would admonish me. "Go on *Howard Stern*! Go, go, go! Think of all the free publicity! You'll get so many people to sign up to your site in one day!"

But I knew I needed to wait until the time was right first.

I gotta step back a little here so I can fully explain the story. As my radio booker Pete would tell you, I really do have a horseshoe up my ass.

How did the King of Radio know who the heck I was in the first place? Pete had this intern on his show back in the Mr. Skin prehistory days. They called him Doogie Howser, because he was this really young kid who had just graduated high school.

Doogie Howser leaves for college and keeps in touch with Pete. Doogie tells Pete he's applying for an internship in New York with Rush Limbaugh. Not exactly Howard Stern, but close.

Pete can't believe this blatant idiocy. Rush Limbaugh? "Come on," Pete tells his former intern. "You love Howard Stern. Let me have my program director give Howard a call and see if he can help you out."

At the time, Pete was syndicating Howard's morning show here in Chicago and thought it might be worth a shot to see if his program director could help Doogie get an internship he could be proud of with one of his idols instead of, well, someone who wasn't.

Lo and behold, Pete's program director gets Doogie Howser an internship with Howard in New York.

Something else that is important here is that Doogie was a *huge* Mr. Skin fan. So, he starts pestering Howard's people to get me on the show. After hectoring everyone he could over the course of his internship, on his way out the door at the end, Doogie had done it: he finally got me invited onto *The Howard Stern Show*.

How lucky is all of *that*?

Still, I instinctively knew that I had to bide my time and go on not only when I was ready, but when the site was ready. If I was going to go on *Howard Stern* and talk about MrSkin.com, I wanted to make sure the millions of people listening would be able to go to a site that could handle the influx of traffic sure to come.

It was that twenty-third day of March 2000 that I finally thought we could do it.

Since that time, I've been on Howard's show at least twenty-five mind-blowing times. It's always a thrill to go into the studio with the king himself. But that first time, I was a call-in guest. It would be the only time I wouldn't go into the studio in person.

Here's an excerpt of how it went:

HOWARD: Mr. Skin is a guy who put together an incredible website. Isn't that right, Mr. Skin? I don't know if Mr. Skin gives out his real name. Do you, Jim?

SKIN: No.

HOWARD: Oh, okay. [laughter] Can I give out that name, though, Jim?

SKIN: It's out there, I guess!

HOWARD: All right. But I'll call you Mr. Skin.

SKIN: Yes.

ROBIN [Howard's co-host]: Mr. Skin has another identity?

HOWARD: Yes.

SKIN: Oh, yeah!

HOWARD: Mr. Skin, how old are you?

SKIN: Thirty-seven.

HOWARD: Okay. And, I'd say for the last twenty years... So, we're talking since he was seven years old...

ROBIN: Seventeen.

HOWARD: Seventeen. Right. I was saying "seven." [laughter]

ROBIN: Seven!

HOWARD: As a hobby, he's been taping movies with nude scenes. And the guy has, like, a photographic memory. You can literally bring up any starlet—

ROBIN: And he will know what movie they did a nude scene in.

HOWARD: Yeah. He will. You're on the air with Mr. Skin. The noted authority on—

ROBIN: The authority!

HOWARD: The authority...on skin.

If you were one of the many people who listened to me on that first show, you would have heard how very, very nervous I was.

Now, I wasn't nervous because I was worrying about wanting to make sure I'd be back on another twenty-four times. I was nervous because I wasn't sure how Howard would react to what I do.

Just like with Harry on my first radio appearance ever, though, Howard couldn't have been nicer. He made me extremely comfortable. He made everything so easy for me. It's a talent of his to make his guests feel great on his show so that they'll have a good time and keep the audience enjoying themselves, too.

Howard *loved* that I knew all this stuff right off the top of my head, that there was this guy out there who put up this website of nude scenes and then went to the trouble of going into such specific detail about them all.

He loved me *so* much that he recommended that all his listeners go check out MrSkin.com for themselves. Which was a good thing and a bad thing.

The good news, of course, was that I got one thousand joins in one day. I don't think I had so many new memberships in the entire six months I had been in operation up to that point. The problem was that I should have gotten *ten* thousand joins.

I thought we had been ready. We weren't. Not really. I was right to have waited as long as I had to go on *Howard Stern*, but there was just no way I could have anticipated how massive it was going to be for our site.

MrSkin.com practically froze under the strain of the traffic bombardment. Me being on *Howard Stern* practically broke the site. To this day, I don't know how I got the thousand joins that *did* thankfully come through. The site was moving like molasses all day. Terrible!

I blame myself. I hadn't invested more into the tech side of our business. What was I supposed to have done? I didn't have the money!

It was a valuable lesson that taught me how important the tech component of what we do at Mr. Skin really is.

I learned something else from my bittersweet *Howard Stern* appearance. I realized I needed to step up my game not only with the business's tech side, but also the *business* side of the business.

In those days, my current CFO Jim K. was only doing some light freelance work for me, helping to organize my books and whatnot. Again, I couldn't afford much more than that.

As Jim K. tells it, "I wasn't super involved at the time, but I do remember that first *Howard Stern* broadcast and looking at how much money Skin made in one day. I couldn't believe these incredible numbers coming in. But Skin was pretty clueless about how to handle the number of subscriptions coming through. *Everyone* was clueless back in the early days of internet commerce."

Something we began figuring out around this time was that you don't bill once and then let the member go. You bill, get their card number, and then have a recurring charge every month.

Then there are trial memberships for maybe three dollars that we can rebill the member for with a thirty- or forty-dollar-a-month charge every month thereafter if they don't cancel.

This became the core of our financial engagement side as it runs today. But Jim K. is right: At the time of that first *Howard Stern* appearance, we *were* clueless. *Everyone* was! It was challenging but fun learning how to build the system together as we watched other internet commerce companies figure out their own similar paths, as well.

Hey, I was six months into playing the game and still had a lot of rules to learn. To add to the pressure, I was realizing guys like *me* were the ones who were having to figure *out* the rules of early internet commerce.

But you know what? Regardless of our fumbles here, I still got to experience the intensely enjoyable sensation of seeing all those thousand people register for MrSkin.com.

"Holy shit!" I remember thinking. "This is unbelievable!"

Plus, I got a ton of calls from friends all over the country who had heard me on the show. That's a rare treat that very few people will ever get to enjoy.

The best part was when I later got a call from Gary Dell'Abate, the producer of *The Howard Stern Show*, who told me that Howard loved having me on so much that he promised I'd be back on. Dell'Abate was as good as his word, and I can tell you that twenty years later, if you were to look at the numbers from my twenty-five biggest business days, twenty of them would be the days I've gone on *Howard Stern*.

I knew what a Skinfining Moment in the history of my company (and life) being on the show would be. I did it: I went on *Howard Stern* for the first time and killed. Even if it practically killed my website for a few brief hours, too!

The Anatomy Awards

I should add that I was on *Howard Stern* to promote my first annual Anatomy Awards, which we started at MrSkin.com in 2000 and debuted on the show.

The Anatomy Awards affectionately puts our own Mr. Skin twist on the *Academy* Awards, timed to come out with the Oscars, annually kicking off on *Howard Stern* before I go to other radio stations and media outlets with our heralded list of winners. It's one of my favorite promotions of the entire Mr. Skin year.

Rather than making fun of the Academy Awards the way, say, the Razzies does their thing, we celebrate all the best nudity in the year's films, TV, and—nowadays—web/mobile series.

What's really cool about the Anatomy Awards is that we get more and more creative with our categories each time we do it. It's nothing to come up with awards for "Best Breast," "Best Butt," "Best TV Show," or "Best Lesbian Scene." It's as easy to crack a joke like "Breast Picture." That's kid stuff.

But what about all the outlandish categories for nudity we come up with that you wouldn't believe exist?

We keep track of all the weirdest scenes from the weirdest movies you've never heard of before. We're very proud of the fact that the Anatomy Awards honor more than just the typical famous films from the year. We shine light on really obscure B movies, TV shows, or online series that may not otherwise get any love. That's where we get some of our funniest categories.

Last year, we had "Best Nude Daughter of a Famous Father: Francesca Eastwood." Pretty specific. But that's what makes the Anatomy Awards so fun to put together. This one made for a good joke, too: "You'll get *north* wood when you see this scene."

How about "Best Milk and Nookie"? Here you might be asking, "*What?*" This category let us showcase a totally obscure mockumentary called *Tour de Pharmacy* where 0:09 minutes in, Eugenia Kuzmina is topless drinking milk while the guy's going down on her. That's fascinating! So, it had to be in our Anatomy Awards.

Then there's "Best Queef."

Okay...*that* one's probably self-explanatory. (And it's *exactly* the kind of thing that always plays so well on *Howard Stern*.) Moving on....

Some of our categories really signal what a bunch of true-blue film fanatics we can be. Like "Best Marty Feldmans." What's a "Marty Feldman"? A Marty Feldman is when a girl's breasts are kind of pointing in different directions.

Feldman, of course, being the primo comedian and actor from such classics as Mel Brooks' *Young Frankenstein* with rather wonky eyes that bulged out of his head in different directions. Just like the boobs upon which we have bestowed his great name.

Victoria Gomez won that skinfamous award for *Peelers* in 2018.

We can get very creative with category names, like "Best Acracknophobia." We used that one for a scene in which Natasha Romanova has a huge spider crawl over her bare ass as she lies on a table at a party in the 2017 thriller *Most Beautiful Island*. It's moments like these that make it all worthwhile, folks.

Probably the proudest I've been of a category we've come up with involved a scene from the STARZ network show *American Gods*. Yetide Badaki is some kind of goddess and has sex with guys...before sucking them into her vagina. The victim ends up flying into the cosmos or universe or whatever—I don't know; I couldn't tell even when I saw the clip.

So, what award did we give it? "Best Vadge-Cuum."

Each awards season, we get together for our year-end meetings and start whittling down the winners to a manageable list. Last year's 120 categories were filtered down to forty-two. (A good number of categories for our page design.)

We'll then have another meeting with my team to go over my "Skin Tales" for each individual movie. These are well-thought-out, researched, and rehearsed backstories I can talk about when I go on radio shows like Howard's, discussing the films on our awards list.

Being the face and voice of the company, I need to know what I'm talking about when I appear on these shows. Since we have so many movies and series to go over, it's a *lot* to talk about. There's no way I'd be able to know everything about the source of a nude scene's plot, storyline, and whatnot, so these Skin Tales allow for some concise blurbs that help me keep abreast of whatever scene I'll be discussing.

Sure, coming up with the award is not science. But we do what we can to ensure we're highlighting all the best and weirdest nude scenes from the year. It can be harder than you'd think, which is why it takes several meetings and all this work to wrap it all up properly.

We sometimes must make tough choices. An indie movie called *Below Her Mouth* has this spectacular scene of the stunning Natalie Krill masturbating using her bath faucet. "Best Masturbation," right? Well...but we already had some "Best Of" scenes from the same film, and we like to spread the awards out so that one movie doesn't end up with, like, five or six. So, we went with the beautiful Karley Sciortino's masturbation scene from the Netflix series *Easy* instead (which was still hot as hell), even though it might not have been quite as good. These are the *very* tough executive decisions I have to make as CSO of Mr. Skin!

My staff makes fun of me because, in the six years *The Americans* aired on FX, I gave "Best Butt" to Keri Russell three times! What can I say? She's got a phenomenal ass. But, in 2018, there was some *stiff* competition, and my team thought she had won the prestigious category enough times. I still won out in the end, because I pointed out that Russell has an amazing "diamond," which she showed off in all of its brilliance on March 14, 2017.

What's a "diamond"? It's a special aspect of the body that very few women possess: the pronounced space between the upper thigh and crack. When I brought up the diamond on *Stern* and other radio shows, we had all these guys listening in their cars or at work wanting to go to our site to check out the clip and see what the heck I was talking about. So, it was worth my getting my way on this one!

Sometimes we'll need to choose a bigger name over a nobody. We're very proud of the fact that we promote these smaller movies and shows people likely haven't heard of before, but we're also running a business and must make sure we mention enough familiar names and faces that will draw in traffic.

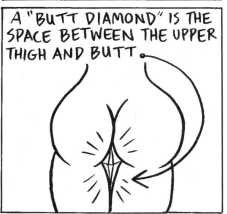

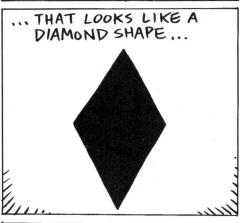

We had this one "Best Lesbian" scene with Sofia Boutella and Charlize Theron that won out, because—yeah, it *was* a terrific lesbian scene…but these are also well-known ladies, and we *are* a *celebrity* nudity site. So, we chose Boutella and Theron over some tough competition, because they're the actresses people will be searching to click on.

TOP FIVE MOST SKINTASTIC LESBIAN SCENES OF ALL TIME

Mr. Skin's picks for the hottest chicks who lick.

5. **Gina Gershon/Jennifer Tilly**—*Bound* (0:19)
4. **Joan Chen/Anne Heche**—*Wild Side* (0:40)
3. **Catherine Deneuve/Susan Sarandon**—*The Hunger* (0:59)
2. **Natalie Krill/Erika Linder**—*Below Her Mouth* (0:49)
1. **Adèle Exarchopoulos/Léa Seydoux**—*Blue is the Warmest Color* (1:20)

TOP FIVE COUGAR/KITTEN LESBIAN SEX SCENES

The hottest Sapphic action between a bold older woman and a younger female bedmate.

5. **Cybill Shepherd/Leisha Hailey**—*The L Word* (S4, Ep4)
4. **Naomi Watts/Sophie Cookson**—*Gypsy* (S1, Ep7)
3. **Cate Blanchett/Rooney Mara**—*Carol* (1:15)
2. **Min-hee Kim/Kim Tae-ri**—*The Handmaiden* (1:39)
1. **Julianne Moore/Amanda Seyfried**—*Chloe* (0:59)

We love to break out our best "Nude Debuts" with the Anatomy Awards, too. Everyone was waiting with salivating anticipation for "Annie" from the show *Community* (actress Alison Brie) to do her first nude scene, and when it finally happened last year, we were so into it at Mr. Skin. And we were obviously not alone!

It's awesome when a famous person we're all waiting on finally does a nude scene. It's a big part of the excitement that surrounds the Anatomy Awards: *Hey, she finally did it! Check her out!*

The award categories are secondary to making sure we choose shots that represent well on computer screens and other devices people use to access our site. That's the most important thing. If people can't see what we're talking about, there's no point in giving the scene/actress an award, even if it's really funny, sexy, or interesting.

This is something worth sneaking in here: whenever I'm asked what's *most* important about a nude scene, I always say, "The lighting."

Seriously, we'll pull scenes out from our Anatomy Awards or elsewhere on the site if the lighting isn't good enough, no matter how fantastic it might otherwise be.

So, while coming up with our Anatomy Awards may not be science, we do take it as seriously as everything else we put together on the site and promote out in the world offline. Which is why someone with such a massive audience and impact as Howard Stern still has us on every year, even two decades after he had me on to talk about them that first time.

Time to Get Normal

Going on *Howard Stern* that first time in 2000 was a giant step in "normalizing" what we do at Mr. Skin.

Look, I *still* get nervous every time I go on the show. Just as we treat everything we do at Mr. Skin as though we're still a struggling start-up needing to prove ourselves every day, every time I go on *Howard Stern*, I feel like I need to do better than my best previous appearance.

Part of this is that they are *consummate* pros over there on Howard's show. His prep staff ask me a ton of really well-researched questions in advance. I'd say that of all the shows I've done and still do, theirs is by far the most thorough preinterview I ever do. I must keep my game up so I can play in their league without striking out.

As a fan of the show, I know how irritating it can be when a guest doesn't do so well or gives a boring interview. So, I put extra pressure on myself as someone who wants to do well not only as the face and voice of my company, but also as a full-fledged fan who doesn't want to flub up Howard's program while I'm on.

In the Court of the King of All Media. Doing the Howard Stern Wrap-Up Show on March 15, 2018. This was mere moments after I shared the main studio with Howard and Robin to announce my 19th annual Anatomy Awards. It's always an honor. (L to R) Jon Hein, Dr. Drew, me, Rahsaan, Gary, Brent, and a producer.

All of this is to say that Howard's show continues to be *the best*. Going on his show is like playing against the Yankees.

Becoming a regular on *Howard Stern* has even had an impact on my private life at home. Howard's longtime partner Robin Quivers once referred to my kids on the show as "Skinfants." My wife and I thought that was so funny, it stuck, and we still call our kids—who are no longer quite so young—Skinfants to this day.

(This went both ways, incidentally. Michelle and I once caught my two daughters playing with their dolls calling one "Howard" and the other "Robin.")

Then there's my sister Kristina. She recalls being a little shy about telling people what it was the company she was starting to work for did when she came on board to work with me full-time. In fact, before I went on *Howard Stern*, she thought she wouldn't stay with us long and was just doing something in the interim of finding another job, helping her brother get his new company up and running.

After the *Howard Stern* appearance, Kristina was out at lunch with a colleague from her former job, and when the friend asked what she was up to, she sheepishly revealed she worked for her brother...a "celebrity nudity expert."

The friend couldn't believe it: "Your brother is Mr. Skin? I just heard him on *Howard Stern!*"

That was the turning point for Kristina. She had never been a big listener of Howard's before, so she hadn't understood at first what a gigantic impact it would have on us. I was still just her brother doing this thing she didn't really take too seriously. Then I'm on *Howard Stern*, and suddenly people are bringing me up more and more in conversations or even asking for merch like Mr. Skin T-shirts.

That's when Kristina decided she'd stick with the job and say it proud: "Yeah, I work for Mr. Skin!"

With so many people knowing who I was now and wanting to get in on the action, I was getting calls left and right to go on more radio shows than ever before.

Over the next few years, I became ubiquitous on radio. I went on *The Bob & Tom Show*, which is a hugely syndicated program. I did a weekly spot on *Don and Mike*, a synidacted afternoon show based out of Washington, DC. I went on Tom Leykis's show, syndicated in the largest markets of all: NYC *and* LA.

Throughout the Los Angeles area, you could hear me all the time on *The Kevin & Bean Show* and *Frosty, Heidi & Frank*. Across Long Island, there I was, doing my thing on *Roger & JP*. I became a regular on plenty of shows in places all around the country: Detroit's *The Drew and Mike Show*, San Francisco's *Lamont & Tony*, Minneapolis' *The 92 KQRS Morning Show* hosted by Tom Barnard, Miami's *The Paul & Young Ron Show*, and many, many others.

In no time at all, after going on *Howard Stern,* I became a frequent guest on radio shows in each of the fifty biggest cities across the country.

This was all I had ever wanted to do: talking about celebrity nudity to as many people as possible. It was fabulous. I was living the dream.

Hanging with Heidi and Frank after dropping by their show on KLOS-FM. How did I only just now think of a joke involving the name "Hide D. Frank"?

My dream. The fact that it also did so much to expand my brand, too, well...that was just icing on the cupcake.

Thank you, Howard.

The Janet Jackson Effect

In 2004, I made more money than all the income I had generated from 1985 (when I graduated college) to 2003 combined.

I still couldn't believe this was all happening for me. But I didn't want to cash in just yet. I wanted to see how much further my luck (and, you know, that hard work I'd put in) would take me. So, I decided to keep investing the money I was making back into the company.

As I said, I had learned an important lesson from that first *Howard Stern* appearance about the need for stronger tech at Mr. Skin. So, the biggest investment I made was in tech people who would help make sure the site wouldn't crash or slow to a standstill again. It turned out to be a decision that paid off right away.

You remember a little thing that happened on February 1, 2004? Super Bowl XXXVIII. Most sports fans probably don't remember who won that year or even who lost. But there is *one* thing *everyone* probably remembers happening during that year's infamous game: Janet Jackson's wardrobe malfunction.

Wholesome pretty boy Justin Timberlake is up there on stage with Jackson, performing in front of the entire world. Live telecast. Right before they cut away to a commercial, as the duo are finishing up their singing and booty shaking, for reasons we'll never know, Timberlake turns to Jackson...and nips at her top, which subsequently falls off, revealing her tit. *Commercial.*

It was a big, big deal.

If you were alive when it happened (and good god, I sincerely hope you were; what are you doing reading this book if you're under fifteen, kiddo?), it's something you'll never forget. Even if you didn't see it live when it happened. It was all over the news for *weeks*, maybe *months* after.

No one was ready for it. How could they be? It wasn't like, "Hey, America, during the Super Bowl halftime show, you're going to see Janet Jackson's breast!" No. That's not how it went down. It just...*happened*. Everyone saw it. And they were *freaking out*.

It's an incident that still has vast resonance over what can and can't be shown on television, how live delays work, and the trajectories of both Jackson's and Timberlake's careers. It was a big, big deal for *everyone*.

Especially big for me.

See, DVRs and TiVos and the rest of that sort of technology hadn't come out yet. So, it wasn't as though people were able to rewind their television and watch the "wardrobe malfunction," unless they were superfans who happen to tape the Super Bowl every year.

As it turned out, there was a guy at the game who had a perfect shot of the moment and, to answer Jackson's own song title—"What Have You Done for Me Lately?"—he thought to email the pic(s) to me, inquiring, "Hey, have you seen these?"

I couldn't believe it. They were fantastic. Hi-res quality and all. He must have been right up front when Jackson's boob burst out for all the world to see during that historical split second. Right away, I put the stills on my website.

The morning after the Super Bowl, the whole world was in a tizzy about what had happened. So much so that people who didn't even know what the Super Bowl was wanted to see for themselves the moment heard round the globe. Not to mention all of those who *had* seen it and wanted a second look.

This was before YouTube. This was before Facebook. This was before TMZ. "God," everyone wondered collectively, "where do you go to find celebrity nudity like this? Where can we see Janet Jackson's breast from the Super Bowl?"

February 2, 2004—the day after that year's Super Bowl—remains our best sign-up day in the history of MrSkin.com.

CONTI-NUDITY ERRORS: NAKED MISTAKES CAUGHT ON CAMERA

As getting naked on screen is never an exact science, bloopers involving butts, boobs, and other body parts have been known to happen. And at Skin Central, of course, we catch every naked bungle! Here are some of my favorites:

- **Beverly D'Angelo**—*National Lampoon's Vacation.* In the full-screen version of her famous shower scene wherein Mrs. Griswold busts out her Natural Pontoons, my Skin Scientists noticed that Bev is actually wearing panties while she washes.

- **Kelly Brook**—*Survival Island.* For about two years in the mid-2000s, Showtime aired the tropical adventure/romance *Survival Island* nonstop during its wee-hour programming schedule. That gave me plenty of time to notice that after Kelly Brook strips to her birthday suit for a skinny-dip, her bikini bottom miraculously re-appears when she comes out of the water.

- **Morena Baccarin**—*Deadpool.* Follow the bouncing tit-too. During a wild montage scene, Morena Baccarin's breast tattoo switches from her left boob to the right.

Our once-in-a-lifetime success on that day didn't come solely from the totally amazing luck of Janet Jackson's tit making its small-screen debut. The success was also due to my having invested properly in the technology and tech staff we needed to make sure the site would work right even if a flash flood of traffic came through, as it did.

Man, the site was humming that day. We nailed it! I was so proud of my team. I know there are a lot of people who, almost twenty years later, are still upset with Janet Jackson and Justin Timberlake for what happened. But all I can say about it is, "Thank you, Miss Jackson!"

TOP FIVE CELEBRITY NIP SLIPS

Accidental appearances by unexpected boob-bulbs.

5. **Tina Fey**—2013 Emmy Awards
4. **Nicki Minaj**—*Good Morning America* (08.05.11)
3. **Lucy Lawless**—*Detroit Red Wings National Anthem* (1997)
2. **Farrah Fawcett**—*Charlie's Angels* (S1, Ep4)
1. **Susan Hayward**—*With a Song in My Heart* (0:48)

TOP FIVE ONE TIT WONDERS

They flashed flesh only once...but it was skintastic!

5. **Kirstie Alley**—*Blind Date* (0:12)
4. **Cindy Morgan**—*Caddyshack* (0:58)
3. **Suzanne Somers**—*Magnum Force* (0:27)
2. **Nicollette Sheridan**—*Raw Nerve* (0:24)
1. **Melinda Dillon**—*Slap Shot* (0:30)

Skinfining Moment #3: Have You Ever Seen *Knocked Up*?

Fast-forward this time to the summer of 2006, and you find yourself at my third "Skinfining Moment."

I get a phone call from an attorney at Universal Studios: "The guy who made *40-Year-Old Virgin* wants to put your website in his next movie."

I brought up the news to a bunch of people I knew, and they all gave me the same sage advice: "Charge the hell out of them!"

I'm listening to everyone trying to tell me how to fleece Judd Apatow and his team with this opportunity, but my instincts were retorting, "Why put any roadblocks in front of them? Why be a pain in the ass? Why sabotage it by making it more trouble than it's worth?"

Against all the well-meaning counsel I received, I said, "You know what? Screw it. Where do I sign?"

I went ahead, went with my gut, and was proud to see MrSkin.com in the movie that came out on June 1, 2007. You may have heard of it: *Knocked Up.*

Here's an excerpt from the scene where we're prominently featured. Seth Rogen's character is talking to Paul Rudd's character about a website he and his friends have been working on that is unwittingly just like MrSkin.com:

PAUL RUDD: *Really? I thought there was a lot of money in porn.*

SETH ROGEN: [sighs] *It's not porn, okay? All we do is, we show what nude scenes are in what movies.*

RUDD: *Well, like Mr. Skin?*

ROGEN: *Who's Mr. Skin?*

RUDD: *Dude, Mr. Skin.* [big Mr. Skin logo smile] *Mr. Skin.* [big smile again]

[Cut to next scene; the boys are at home looking at a computer screen with the Mr. Skin website onscreen]

JONAH HILL: *No! We wasted fourteen months of our lives!*

ROGEN: *This is exactly the same as our site. How the fuck did this happen?*

HILL: *"Mr. Skin"! That's even a better name than ours!*

MARTIN STARR: *Fuck me in the beard.*

JASON SEGEL: Dude, they've got the "Top Ten Shower Scenes"!
   Why didn't you think of that, Jay?

JAY BARUCHEL: Don't put this on me!

ROGEN: Goddamn it.

STARR: Well, shit. I saw it online at one point, but I guess I
   didn't connect the dots.

HILL: What are we going to do now?

So, how did *this* happen? How did I luck into having my website in what would end up becoming one of the Top Ten Movies of the Year according to the American Film Institute and, as time has told, would become one of the most beloved and critically acclaimed movies of the entire decade?

Apatow is a longtime Howard Stern fan. He was trying to figure out what kind of ridiculous, crappy job his main character Ben (eventually

This guy tried to rip off my website—you know, in a movie! Amazed to be with Seth Rogen at the Hollywood premiere of *Knocked Up* (2007).

played by Rogen) could have in *Knocked Up*. Apparently, Apatow wanted to make sure it was something *super* embarrassing, so it would be funny whenever Ben brought it up to people in the film.

Of course, Apatow chose having Ben do what I do at MrSkin.com. Perfect!

Apatow told me this story after he invited my wife and I to the premiere of *Knocked Up*. He turned out to be a really nice guy, as was Rogen and the rest of the team involved in the film. Everyone was really cool to my wife and me at the screening, took pictures with us, and made us feel like we were part of the production.

Apatow's young daughters are there, both because their dad made the movie and because they're in it. He calls them over to take pictures with me and his whole family, including his wife and actress (also in the film) Leslie Mann. Apatow's cracking up, telling the kids, "You don't understand why this is so funny now, but you will some day!" I still have those pictures in my office.

It was pretty cool that they let me bring Michelle along, but this makes sense considering she's *Mrs.* Skin. You know what else she was that night? *Very* pregnant.

Knocked Up, as you undoubtedly already know, is about this young stoner loser Rogen plays who accidentally gets this young lady on the rise in the news business—played by the lovely and talented Katherine Heigl—pregnant. The film casts a hilarious lens on how this literal odd couple deal with their situation.

Michelle and I go to the premiere's after-party, and we walk inside... to find all the waitresses wearing these fake baby bumps. Michelle's standing there with the *real thing* under her dress. Annnnnnd...*scene*.

The particularly awesome thing about the product placement of MrSkin.com in *Knocked Up* isn't just that the characters say the name of our site and put us on display on their computer at a memorable, critical juncture in the film. It's also the fact that Apatow had his characters laboring over their own version of MrSkin.com for so long—more than a year, according to Hill's character—and yet as soon as they see my site, they're like, "We give up! There's no way we can compete."

I've joked in the past that the only better product placement was for Reese's Pieces in *E.T.*

Knocked Up ended up raking in an astounding 250 million dollars that summer and has probably aired more than five thousand times across such networks and cable channels as E!, TBS, TNT, and plenty more, continuously, since 2007. What a terrific way to get the word out about our site: our traffic went up 35 percent after the movie came out.

People who would have never thought to look us up were finding out about Mr. Skin, and you can't put a price on that kind of universal publicity.

Pete still remembers the *Knocked Up* gold rush, when all at once the phones were ringing off the hook, with radio stations around the country wanting me to come on their shows: "Skin was booked all over the United States. He was doing TV, radio, everything. It was great. It was big."

When your website is in a movie of this magnitude, a film that has such a wide-spanning cultural relevance, that website *also* ends up becoming ingrained in pop culture history forevermore. Prior to *Knocked Up*, we were mostly confined to the "adult" industry. Which I'm okay with. It is what it is. Or, should I say, it *was* what it *was*. Because after *Knocked Up*, we were now in the mainstream, too.

Isn't It Porn?

All of us at Mr. Skin are well aware of what it is we do. None of us are laboring under any kind of grand delusions. But we do believe in our product and the work we put into making it the highest quality.

We *are* adding something to the pop culture zeitgeist. I'd even like to think that some of our "Skinfinitions" or jokey terms we use for certain body parts, sexual positions, or fetishes have contributed to the collective cultural lexicon. It's certainly added to the online one!

At the same time, these conversations like the one in *Knocked Up* between Rudd's and Rogen's characters are familiar territory for us at the office: *Isn't what we're doing just porn?*

The scene in *Knocked Up* is a brilliant moment of art (unknowingly) imitating art, according to Michelle: "I told Judd Apatow I felt that he was in my brain while he was writing some of those scenes. I literally almost peed my pants when Katherine Heigl's character says at one point, 'It's not porn! It's R-rated!' I say that at least three times a week!"

THE STRIP

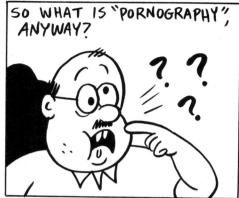

SO WHAT IS "PORNOGRAPHY", ANYWAY?

ARE PICTURES IN "NATIONAL GEOGRAPHIC" OF INDIGENOUS PEOPLES IN AFRICA BEING TOPLESS OR NUDE "PORNOGRAPHY"?

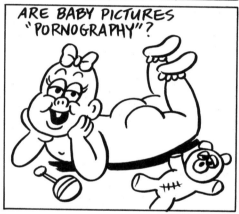

ARE BABY PICTURES "PORNOGRAPHY"?

ARE BEAUTIFULLY SKETCHED PAINTINGS OR DRAWINGS OF NUDE PERSONS "PORNOGRAPHY"?

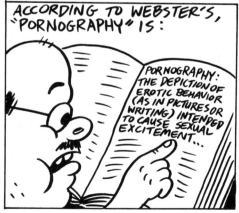

ACCORDING TO WEBSTER'S, "PORNOGRAPHY" IS:

PORNOGRAPHY: THE DEPICTION OF EROTIC BEHAVIOR (AS IN PICTURES OR WRITING) INTENDED TO CAUSE SEXUAL EXCITEMENT...

BOY, DOES THIS DEFINITION GET COMPLICATED...

AS WE'RE SEEING MORE & MORE THESE DAYS...

SOMETHING THAT WAS AT ONCE CONSIDERED "ART"...

OR THAT HAD AN AESTHETIC OR EVEN HISTORICAL/CONTEXTUAL MERIT AT ONE POINT...

MIGHT NOW BE SEEN AS "OFFENSIVE" OR "PORNOGRAPHIC" THRU THE LENS OF MODERN PERSPECTIVE.

SO WHO DECIDES THIS?

THE PRESIDENT?

OPRAH?

MARK ZUCKERBERG?

THE POPE?

AEROSMITH?

IN 1964, THERE WAS A NOTORIOUS SUPREME COURT CASE --- JACOBELLIS V. OHIO.

IT WAS DURING THIS CASE THAT JUSTICE POTTER STEWART FAMOUSLY EXPLAINED THAT A PARTICULAR FILM WAS NOT "OBSCENE"....

AND THAT NO SCENE IN IT— EXPLICIT SEX OR NOT— WAS TO BE CONSIDERED "HARDCORE PORNOGRAPHY"...

WHICH WAS TO BE DEFINED AS "I KNOW IT WHEN I SEE IT."

IN AN EFFORT TO BE SLIGHTLY MORE CLEAR ABOUT ALL OF THIS, JUSTICE STEWART'S "I KNOW IT WHEN I SEE IT" DECLARATION WAS AMENDED SOMEWHAT THRU THE 1966 CASE MEMOIRS V. MASSACHUSETTS...

THIS WAS THE CASE WHOSE VERDICT DICTATED THE SLIGHTLY MORE SPECIFIC NOTION THAT TO BE "PORNOGRAPHY" THE MATERIAL IN QUESTION MUST:

... BE PATENTLY OFFENSIVE, APPEALING TO PRURIENT INTEREST AND HAVE NO REDEEMING SOCIAL VALUE!

HMM. THAT'S STILL A LITTLE VAGUE, ISN'T IT?

WHICH IS WHY IN 1973, THERE WAS YET ANOTHER CASE THAT HELPED MAKE THINGS A LITTLE MORE CLEAR TO LOWER COURTS ACROSS THE LAND...

THE CASE WAS MILLER V. CALIFORNIA...

POW!

PORN MAG

CALI

AND LED TO A MORE SPECIFIC TEST CALLED, APTLY, THE MILLER TEST.

QUIET TESTING IN PROGRESS

THE SUPREME COURT DETAILED MATERIAL THAT WAS TO BE REGULATED BY STATE OR OTHER LOWER COURTS/ARBITRATION WOULD HAVE TO MEET THREE CRITERIA:

THE AVERAGE PERSON, APPLYING LOCAL COMMUNITY STANDARDS, LOOKING AT THE WORK IN ITS ENTIRETY, MUST FIND THAT IT APPEALS TO THE PRURIENT INTEREST...

PHONE BOOK

THE WORK MUST DESCRIBE OR DEPICT, IN AN OBVIOUSLY OFFENSIVE WAY, SEXUAL CONDUCT...

OR EXCRETORY FUNCTIONS.

THE WORK AS A WHOLE MUST LACK "SERIOUS LITERARY, ARTISTIC, POLITICAL, OR SCIENTIFIC VALUES."

THE 3RD CRITERION PERTAINS TO JUDGEMENT MADE BY "REASONABLE PERSONS" OF THE UNITED STATES AS A WHOLE...

WHILE THE FIRST TWO PERTAIN TO THAT OF MEMBERS OF THE LOCAL COMMUNITY.

STILL PRETTY SUBJECTIVE, YOU SAY? YUP. BUT THAT'S "PORNOGRAPHY" FOR YA!

When the question of what he does for a living crops up, Alberto (a.k.a. Be) in our content department might just say he's a video editor and leave it at that. If the conversation keeps going and he doesn't think whomever he's talking with won't get "offended," Be might go the full monty: "I work for Mr. Skin," which sometimes does lead the stranger to ask, "So…it's porn?"

For many of my employees, Mr. Skin is not porn, because we only traffic in mainstream material. We don't really upload clips and stills from adult films, just from movies and TV shows produced by legit Hollywood/indie studios, networks, and streaming services.

When asked if *he* thought Mr. Skin is porn, Doc—one of my designers—had this to say: "I don't really see Winona Ryder doing a lot of double penetration. So, no."

You want *my* honest opinion on all of this? I personally have nothing against porn. Believe me, over the past few years, we've tried everything to get more substantial mainstream partners and advertisers involved in what we do. It finally dawned on me, though: *fuck it.* If we're going to work with partners in the porn industry like Vivid or some of the cam sites we're linked to, what's the big deal? Their money is as green as everybody else's.

Remember: fifty employees. I want to make sure we can make as much money as we can, and if the porn folks are more apt to work with us and support us and *make us that money* than Budweiser or some other mainstream company operating under the misconception that we're porn, why not go with them?

A Hard Day's Work

Just as they think we're porn peddlers at Mr. Skin, a lot of people out there might think we're a bunch of creepy degenerates in Mom's basement, sweating over nude scenes in movie after movie, show after show.

I'm here to set the record straight. That's only *partly* true. In truth, as my managing editor Vera has put it, we're mostly a bunch of mild-mannered nerds and geeks.

Those same mistaken critics out there might be equally surprised to learn that the adult industry itself can be a lot nicer and more welcoming than the mainstream media and entertainment industries.

The adult industry is a much smaller niche, so—as is the case with us at the Mr. Skin office—it's its own little community. People know each other in that business, and for the most part take care of one another.

When you go to an adult industry business conference, it's basically the same two or three thousand people. They stick to what they do in that field and at their companies. In the mainstream game, meanwhile, there's a much higher turnover with people always coming and going, shifting gears, and switching positions rapidly. So, when you go to *those* conferences or meetups, you never know who's doing what, and you might have no idea who the person is you're talking to, because the person who did his or her job last year is no longer doing it.

I'm sure it's no startling revelation that Hollywood itself hasn't exactly been that kind to its own people over the years. Beyond all the torrid stories and admissions of guilt about inappropriate behavior popping up so often these days, there's also a lot of scammers and moochers in Hollywood and the rest of the mainstream media/entertainment realm who will take advantage of you. Believe it or not, this is not something that happens quite so often in the adult industry.

I've been to more than twenty AVN Awards shows—the Academy Awards of the adult industry. I've been on Playboy TV with girls pressing their breasts against my face. I've been to the Playboy Mansion. I've been around a *lot* of nakedness in my day.

I don't want to say I'm numb to it, because you can never get fully numb to it. But I think, over time, it simply becomes part of what we do, the way no one at my office raises an eyebrow when they walk by someone's computer and see a girl pleasuring a guy underwater in a swimming pool on the screen.

Some time after we took over *Naked News*, a web series that is exactly what you think it is, my company president Sam and I went over to their office in Toronto to find—not surprisingly—one of their lead anchors completely nude. She saw me coming in and went right up to me to give me a big, warm, welcoming hug.

I'm thinking to myself, "How many guys in the course of their regular workday get to be hugged by a completely naked woman without getting into any kind of trouble?"

So, yeah, it's a cool perk. But I'm married. Happily. And this is how it is for everyone at the office: It's a job. A cool job. An incredible job. But a job nonetheless. It's still an office, and we treat it that way.

Wait, You Work at Mr. Skin?

I gotta say, sometimes the misunderstandings about what we do at Mr. Skin can be a *good* thing. For one thing, this confusion about who and what we are led us to ending up with our fantastic production manager, Christian. He's become one of the most vital members of our team. That he initially thought we were porn—a fascinating development to him— is why he found out about who we were in the first place.

It was right around when *Knocked Up* came out, so we were only then starting to really make a dent in the mainstream culture. Christian still had no idea who or what Mr. Skin was. He's hanging out at his usual watering hole when he hears the bartender call out to someone at the other end of the counter, "Hey, Porno Guy! What'll you have?"

Christian turns to "Porno Guy" and asks what's with the name. As it happened, Christian was talking with one of our early employees, who explained what his job *actually* was—a cut-and-dry programming gig for a "database of nudity in television and film" (the usual boilerplate)— and that the bartender loved ribbing him for being in "porn."

If the bartender *hadn't* made the crack, Christian wouldn't have been so intrigued as to lean over and engage with the programming guy, wouldn't have found out through the same person that there was an opening in the tech department, and wouldn't have become one of our best hires to date.

"The site sounded hilarious," Christian recalls thinking once he understood what it was we do at Mr. Skin. "And, you know, I was doing freelance at the time, so a steady job sounded nice. I was in!"

Due to this confusion about what it is we do at Mr. Skin, one of the big questions that comes up a lot for my employees is whether friends and family are cool with their working for the company.

It's rare that my guys receive a negative reaction when they reveal where they work to the people in their lives.

For one thing, it's easy for them to say something like, "I work for a media company that produces compilations and short videos." Simple.

They can expand on how we put together promotions that, along with our renowned playlists, include our "Mr. Skin Minute." You've already been reading some of our playlists and have seen them on our site if you're a fan of Mr. Skin already. But the Mr. Skin Minutes are these short audio clips that we do every week that used to be played on *Howard Stern* and Playboy TV.

These days, they're mostly for our own site and partner entities, but we still produce them with the same quality of professional craftsmanship as we had in the days when they went out to Howard.

What we do is pick three highlights from the week's news in noteworthy nudity: a newly released movie with lots of nakedness in it, or maybe something from the "real" news involving a scandal with a politician and a stripper. Then people like our managing editor Vera and our associate editor Steve and I come up with amusing ways to relay these highlights to our audience.

We're basically crowdsourcing the lines we're going to say the way they bounce ideas around in a sitcom writers' room.

Here's an excerpt from an actual brainstorming session we (writers, editors, and myself) had, deliberating over how to announce the recent Blu-ray release of the 1992 Penelope Cruz/Javier Bardem film *Jamón Jamón* (which, by the way, means "*Ham Ham*"):

BETH: *"Nude for the first time on Blu-ray, Penelope Cruz's nude debut in 1992's Jamón Jamón. Penelope is eighteen here and shows her stuffed Spanish olives in four scenes, with her future husband, Javier Bardem. Looks like this jamon is bone-in!"*

SKIN: *Oooh!*

STEVE: *"Nude on Blu-ray, catch up with Penelope Cruz's screen debut in the newly remastered 1992 flick, Jamón Jamón. The scenes of Penelope's future relationship with Javier Bardem show the two Spaniards getting down to some porking. Jamón Jamón will make you H.A.M. for business!"*

SKIN: *Very good.*

VERA: *"Nude on Blu-ray is Penelope Cruz's feature film debut in 1992's Jamón Jamón. See eighteen-year-old Penelope Cruz in glorious HD, as she strips down in four steamy scenes with Javier Bardem. Forget ham: Penelope will please your sausage."*

BETH: *I think all of Steve's is very funny.*

VERA: *'Cause the "porking"?*

BETH: *Why did I not think of "porking"?!*

SKIN: *Do people know that jamón means "ham" in Spanish?*

BETH: *I think they'll figure it out.*

VERA: *I think so.*

BETH: *I think so, too.*

VERA: *It's so close to "ham" in pronunciation, too.*

STEVE: *I don't know who came up with this, but on our website for the film, the alternative title is listed as A Tale of Ham and Passion.*

SKIN: *Oh, really?*

BETH: *A tale of ham and passion!*

STEVE: *I don't know whose doing that was, but that's one of the aliases for the title.*

VERA: *I feel like there were a few things in the olden days where it was so real, like sometimes there would be these fake alternative titles put in. Skin?*

BETH: *I'm pushing for all of Steve's.*

SKIN: *Mmmm...*

BETH: *I would change "screen debut" to "nude debut," just to drive home that she's naked.*

SKIN: *Yeah.*

VERA: *Not sure if it's her debut.*

BETH: *I think it's her first movie. Ever.*

SKIN: She's eighteen in this, so...

BETH: She did some TV show before.

VERA: Oh, she did? But was she nude in it?

BETH: Yes.

VERA: Oh.

SKIN: Well, but when did that show come out?

VERA: I can't tell, because we have only the years when the TV show was on over its entire duration. I don't know when she might have been nude in an episode.

BETH: Well, there's an easy fix: we can keep "screen debut" and say, "The two Spaniards get down to some naked porking."

VERA: Sure.

SKIN: Hold on. I think if it is her nude debut, I just want to make sure of the timeline. [looks at computer screen] I don't like the way our website lays this out anymore.

BETH: Yeah, I always want it in list form, where I can search from first to last.

SKIN: Yeah. [pauses, looks at computer] Yeah, let's just say it's an "early nude."

BETH: Okay.

SKIN: Or something to that effect.

VERA: "Catch Penelope Cruz's early nudes in newly remastered 1992 flick Jamón Jamón!"

SKIN: Yeah.

VERA: All right.

SKIN: "Jamón Jamón will make you H.A.M. for this movie. Yeah, okay."

No matter what other people outside of the office think about us, we do take what we do seriously! So, why wouldn't we be proud of what we do at Mr. Skin?

This flows over into my personal life, too. My wife Michelle likes to tell of the time she came home after I'd been gone for a business trip and was already asleep. I was totally exhausted because I'd been in Vegas for a long conference, and I'd left some sex toy demos that I'd been given on the counter in the kitchen and just went right to bed.

Michelle gets home, sees seven sex toys of various sizes, colors, and shapes on the kitchen counter right there next to the dirty dishes and opened boxes of crackers, and she does what makes the most sense: she takes a picture of this lascivious tableau on her phone and sends them to all her friends with the text, "This is my life."

What did her friends do? Did they get upset? Were they disgusted? Did they ask her why the hell she would send such a picture? No. More like, "Wow, can I have the one on the left?"

You'll remember that Michelle and I had only just started dating when I was first getting the site up and running. She was back home for a holiday or something with her family in Michigan when she announced to her dad and three brothers that she had met someone and that it was getting serious.

They of course asked what it was I did, and Michelle reluctantly confessed that "he has this website called Mr. Skin...and you can go on it and look up any actress to see if they've been naked in a movie."

Literally *half a second later*, all four of these hot-blooded males fly over to the computer to look up MrSkin.com. They're crowding around the screen, having a ball on the site.

"Oh," Michelle says to a table of now empty chairs. "I guess you're okay with it, then?"

Five years later, Michelle's brother was working for me in tech. He ended up going to work at *Playboy*, but to this day, Michelle and I have never had problems with friends and family finding out what it is I do for a living.

Christian has the best story when it comes to such an experience. It was right after he first heard about us through "Porno Guy" and interviewed with Sam and our director of operations Ryan.

Christian's girlfriend and he are driving on their annual "Southern Tour" through Atlanta and North Carolina, where their respective families live, for the holidays. It's while driving that Christian gets the call from Ryan that he can have the job at Mr. Skin if he wants it. Christian says he'll take it, right before his girlfriend and he pull into his family's garage in North Carolina.

Into the house they go to find Christian's mom and sister watching TV in the living room. They all greet each other—hugs and kisses—and shortly after, Christian and his girlfriend are making some food for themselves in the kitchen because they're hungry after the long drive.

That's when they overhear Christian's mom and sister laughing about what they can also hear blaring off the TV set: *Knocked Up*. It's the scene when the boys in the film are angrily talking about Mr. Skin.

Christian and his girlfriend exchange a look: *What now?* All he had told his mother was that he just got a job for a "graphic design company" to spare her any possible concerns she might otherwise have had if she found out he worked for a celebrity nudity website.

Later that evening, Christian's talking with his sister and reveals to her, "You know that scene in the movie with Mr. Skin?"

"Yeeeaaaahhhh...?"

"*That's* the job I got."

"*Shut the fuck up!*"

Christian and his sister are busting up about it, and he realized how silly it was of him to try to keep the job from his family. Even if they *are* North Carolinians.

Southerners or not, Christian's mom and dad took the news easily. Actually, they found it totally hilarious. And, hey, their son was about to start working for the company from the movie *Knocked Up!*

True, just because we're on *Howard Stern* all the time and in a huge movie like *Knocked Up*, that doesn't mean *everyone* will know who we are when you say, "I work for Mr. Skin." Our office administrator Lisa can tell you that we still get phone calls from people who think "Mr. Skin" is a day spa. Or a dermatologist.

But, it's due to our featured placement in these pop culture jewels—now including shows like *Saturday Night Live*, *Entourage*, and *Californication*—that we definitely have a fan base that loves what we do and continues to be on the rapid grow.

I have to say, though, it was *Knocked Up* that really paved the way for us to be included in so many of these other projects over the past few years and helped usher us toward a level of brand awareness that we may not have otherwise been able to reach. Which is just an amazing, amazing thing.

Thanks, Judd.

CLIMAX

SUCCESS AND THE (SK)INNER WORKINGS OF MR. SKIN

Wild Style

You know what else is an amazing, amazing thing? How much has changed over the past twenty years. For me. For MrSkin.com. For the internet.

In the beginning of Mr. Skin, it was just me in my little studio apartment pounding out these reviews and bios on my own. Then I received some assistance from a few friends and my sister Kristina.

From there, we expanded the operation to an actual office in Chicago's Oak Park, where I had grown up. It was a brief period that those of us who were there still refer to as the "Wild West days." People were smoking pot in the office out in the open. That kind of thing. Fun times all day long.

Sure, we were working as hard as ever. But things were a lot looser at our early Oak Park office. We even had a bathroom that was exclusively for smokers. Sam remembers working in the content department before he moved up the corporate ladder to become company president: they were right by that bathroom—with practically no windows around to air out the smoke. The tiny bathroom included an even tinier

Skin Celebration 2006. That's me in the back middle of this mess of skinployee madness. A lot of these people still work for me, but now they have families and get some sleep!

ashtray, so there would just be piles and piles of filthy ash on the floor. Sam's glad we moved on.

One of our marketing guys in those days would smoke weed *all day*. He'd be puffing away, playing on his bongos. Yes, he had a set of bongo drums in his office. That we could all hear. All the time.

It was a totally different animal back then.

A lot of those wild times overlapped into the larger location we moved to a few years later in Chicago's north-side hipster haven known as Wicker Park.

Our creative director Dan remembers a summer party we had at our Wicker Park office that ended up becoming extra-special for his wife-to-be Jackie (who also works for us) and him. It was 2011, and Dan and Jackie were about to be married. We had brought in some strippers to keep things as steamy as we knew people would expect for a Mr. Skin shindig.

Because this was Wicker Park and *not* Oak Park, we wanted to observe *some* professional decorum. So, we declared: "No lap dances! Absolutely not!" But…we also wanted to celebrate Dan and Jackie's forthcoming nuptials. So, we set them down somewhere in the back of the office, away from everyone else, and proceeded to get *them* the only permissible lap dances on the premises.

Obviously the secret got out, and the whole company filed into the back area to watch Dan and Jackie's wedding gift in all its glory. It turned out to be our young content manager Joey's first time seeing a stripper. Heck, it was the first "company party" he'd ever been to in his short-lived career.

We would also throw these madcap rooftop parties that would go on all night. The nail in the coffin on *those* babies was probably the time the fire marshal came to shut us down.

Actually, no, wait. *First*, there were the police detectives who came storming in. They were *followed* by the fire marshal. It's possible we may have tipped them off by our projecting clips of nudity from our favorite movies all over the street below and across to the sides of neighboring buildings up and down Damen Avenue.

Total pandemonium. And total fun.

We used to have parties all the time. We didn't need an anniversary or a holiday to rock out and get crazy. In fact, we *still* get together at the office for some good times revolving around the start of the Major League Baseball playoffs. Still the same parties, just without getting shut down by the authorities, without the requisite photocopying of our asses on the copy machines, and we normally have booze left over the day after. It's hard to drink like you're in your twenties and thirties when you're in your forties and fifties.

Along with the hangovers being harsher now that we're all older, the parties themselves are much more intimate and chill. We'll even have meetups the next day sometimes to all clean up together, guzzling down the leftover kegs and finishing up half-full bottles of liquor. The cleanups can be almost as fun as the parties themselves!

"The people who have been here the longest have been here for fifteen years in many cases," my director of operations Ryan says. "We've all been maturing and growing up and treating the job with a little more seriousness. Jim has put in so much blood, sweat, and tears, and so we began to follow suit, adapting to the changing times and growing up…a little. Some companies don't make that transition. But, we did."

Ch-Ch-Ch-Changes

I really have changed a lot over the years, too.

As my company president Sam will tell you, my passion for celebrity nudity has some new rivals. Like my kids, especially when they have baseball games.

"But he can still talk about celebrity nudity for *hours* without getting bored of it," Sam continues. "And he's still passionate about keeping up with everything that's going on at the company."

I'm still pretty much the same guy I've always been. Hey, I created an entire company that allowed me to totally indulge myself in this weird thing I loved even as a teenager. But let's just say I also no longer wear the obnoxiously bright and gauche Hawaiian shirts that made for my uniform back in my days at the Merc when "Mr. Skin" was still just my secret identity on the radio.

I've *never* been the preppy guy wearing yacht shoes and a blue blazer. I *did* have to wear a tie at the Merc, and being me, I'd only don a skinny tie-dyed belt that I'd rigged to *look* like a real tie. I wasn't allowed to wear jeans, but I could wear khakis. And comfortable gym shoes.

I did have a certain fashion during my Mr. Skin prehistory. It was just, you know, totally horrible and *cheap.*

My outrageous Hawaiian shirts may have let me feel more like an individual and were far more comfortable than the typical button-up shirt…but my wife was *horrified* by them. They were practically a deal-breaker when we first started going out.

I'd meet up with her for our dates wearing these Jams World Hawaiian shirts with the ratty, worn-in jeans I wasn't allowed to wear at the Merc, and Michelle finally put her foot down (right on my gym shoes!): "*No more Hawaiian shirts, Jim!*"

I've since graduated to wearing John Varvatos because, well, it's John Varvatos.

What can I say? I like to look nice. And I'm ever grateful that, these days, I have the ability to wear things that would have been unreachably expensive beforehand.

When I started this business, I couldn't afford anything remotely close to John Varvatos. You'll remember that I could barely afford dinner. So, six-hundred-dollar boots or a fifteen-hundred-dollar coat I might be drooling over in the store window? No way.

I've tried to sneak in a Hawaiian shirt here or there, but those same kids of mine who now make fun of me for my John Varvatos compulsion (not to mention Michelle) strictly prohibit them. We went to the *actual* Hawaii two years ago, and I told my family I wanted to buy a new Jams World shirt. They all called back at me, embarrassed: "No!"

So, I stick to my John Varvatos. Even if my kids do make fun of me for that, too. At least I look a little better while they point and laugh.

Teched Out

I never dared dream I would ever wear that brand of high-class apparel until success hit us right in the balls at Mr. Skin. A sport coat costing more than my earlier rent for the month? No way.

It's nice that we can *all* enjoy the fruit of our labors these days. We want to keep alive a strong company that might be fun to work at but that can also continue to support our fifty-person employee pool.

We do maintain a relatively easygoing atmosphere at the Mr. Skin office. But, adaptation is a defining feature of how we continue to flourish year after year. And that means our continuing to grow up, becoming more sophisticated in what we're attempting to accomplish, and giving up childish things (*cough cough: like Hawaiian shirts*) for more mature investments (like our more strategic member subscription system).

"If you want to stay relevant and continue to make money with a company like this," our production manager Christian suggests, "you *have* to evolve."

He's not the only employee of mine who essentially sees us as a straight-up "tech company." (This depends on who you talk to, by the way; our designer Doc sees us as an "art form"...but then again, he's an artist, so I guess it's all subjective!)

It's so critical to our well-being that we keep up-to-date with all the latest apps, software, devices, and other technological trends.

Sam and I still laugh about the first few years of Mr. Skin, when he started with us. He might be our president now, but back when he first came onboard in 2001, he was working as a Skintern fresh off a stint in Spain, just after finishing college at my own alma mater of Indiana U. He was living in Chicago, DJ-ing and doing some videography work.

He had met a friend who worked for us and who brought him in—a familiar origin story here at Mr. Skin for many of our employees. Sam and his friend were "boob-counting" as Skinterns in the content department: watching, pulling clips and stills from movies and TV shows, before tagging and uploading them to our system.

Though Sam's friend left to pursue his art career in New York City, Sam had met a girl here in Chicago, stuck around for her, and the rest is history.

He was soon getting paid ten dollars a pop to make collages of movie stills and DVD box tops he cropped for us. The part that makes us laugh is how god-awful the resolution quality was back then. We were literally just pulling clips and stills from an Avid machine—which filmmakers used and sometimes still use to edit their movies—that we'd load up with flick after flick and television series after series from mostly crappy VHS tapes and (if we were lucky) standard-def DVDs.

We'd end up with these shittily interlaced screen caps that were often very pixelated and slightly distorted.

We'd have to mess around with the sizing of the images Sam was using to produce his ten-dollar collages, a lot of times blending together multiple shots out of *necessity* as much as for creativity and promotional sakes. If we could blend certain stills together just right, no one would notice how crappy the original individual images were.

Sam later revealed to me that throughout this wobbly dalliance with low-grade tech, he had no idea at first how to use Photoshop. He had in fact, er, "embellished" his rather modest skill set during the interview to get the job.

Luckily, aside from having a terrific "gift for fiction," he was a fast learner. In fact, he got so adept at cranking out these collages that we were beginning to cut him these huge checks. We soon had to cut back: five dollars per collage. A little while later, I realized just how adept he was at a *lot* of things and he eventually rose up in the ranks to become president and run the company with me.

It's still maybe the most important part of what we do to keep things running smoothly at Mr. Skin: working on ensuring our staff is keeping up with the current technology so that both they and we can keep making giant leaps forward.

It's why we keep supporting our tech staff like our wunderkind QA (quality assurance) specialist Ian in attending all the conferences, meetups, and classes they can find to broaden their scope of knowledge. It benefits them, and it benefits the company.

"I like learning all sorts of tech stuff," Ian says. "If there's an event in Chicago, especially if it's free, I'll go to it. You get to do a lot of networking, too. Oh, and they usually have free food…and beer."

Stayin' Alive

How can a pay site like MrSkin.com continue to churn out enviable profits and get all this notice and airtime on radio shows, podcasts, TV shows, and movies day after day, week after week, and year after year at a time when there's so much free stuff online everywhere?

It's a valid question to ask, and one that comes up in almost every interview that I do. Especially these days when there's *sooooo much free content online.*

There are plenty of reasons that MrSkin.com not only survives but evolves and expands in the current freebie online economic climate.

First off: *I'm Mr. Skin.*

Okay. You're wondering if I've totally lost it. Of *course* I'm Mr. Skin. You're halfway through an entire book about my being Mr. Skin.

But what does being Mr. Skin *mean* when it comes to answering the all-too-important question of how we keep making so much money even when humongous juggernauts like YouTube and Twitter struggle to turn a profit.

By declaring "I'm Mr. Skin," I mean that there is a (friendly) face behind the business, behind the name, behind the site. Get it? There's someone you feel like you know personally when you come to my site. Rather like the whole fascination with celebrity itself that I was elaborating upon earlier on in my story.

Mr. Skin isn't just a site someone can use to explore the domain of celebrity nudity. It's also a place where this wacky guy with this unfathomable gift for knowledge about this field can take you on a trip you can't really find anywhere else, at least not in the same detailed, amusing, and interactive way.

It's as though I'm taking all the millions of people who check us out on a regular basis back to Charlie's Ale House or the Eurodollar pit at the Chicago Mercantile Exchange, and they're the ones now cracking up at all this nonsense spewing out of my brain.

More importantly, I'm not alone here. My staff too has proven that we're *all* of us the kind of slap-you-on-the-back-at-the-bar type of buddies people want to check in with, listen to, and witness what crazy stuff they conjure up next through our exclusive videos, podcasts, interviews, reviews, and special promotions like our Anatomy Awards. What we do at Mr. Skin goes way beyond the poorly edited clips and low-rent, random screenshots you'll find elsewhere.

People do connect with me, with us, with Mr. Skin. My bright and chipper office administrator Lisa, who also handles the bulk of our customer service, knows this to be true because she's the one fielding all our calls and emails.

Lisa has handled some pretty ridiculous correspondence from fans over the years, as you could guess. This is a typical question you can expect to receive if you work in customer service at our company:

> *I'm looking for a particular movie that I have no idea how to describe other than it's black-and-white and probably from the sixties. If you know it, I'm more than willing to become a member. All I know is that the man and woman get in a fight at the very end, and he pushes her in the water and rips her top off. Google search of this movie has come up with nothing for me, so I'm hoping you guys know what I'm talking about.*

(It was notable cinematic hooter hero Russ Meyer's *Mudhoney*, featuring a scene with Lee Ballard at the end.)

TOP FIVE NUDE SCENES IN BLACK-AND-WHITE

Naked heat is a color all its own.

5. **Valerie Perrine**—*Lenny* (0:14)
4. **Carla Gugino**—*Sin City* (0:16)
3. **Cybill Shepherd**—*The Last Picture Show* (0:39)
2. **Andrea Thompson**—*A Gun, a Car, a Blonde* (1:08)
1. **Jayne Mansfield**—*Promises, Promises* (0:59)

Some fans will tell us things most people would only confess to their closest friends. Or priest. Or therapist. It's as though these people believe we really are here for *them* and them alone. And you know what? In a lot of ways, we are. It's an intimate relationship we are able to cultivate with our fan base at Mr. Skin.

By the way, these sometimes outrageous confessionals don't stop on the site. They follow us—my employees and myself—into the realm of the offline world, too. I might be at a cocktail party or dinner, and as soon as new people find out what I do, they can't *wait* to declare all this insane stuff about their sexual fetishes.

I'll be picking up the kids from Sunday school at our synagogue, and some congregant will come rushing up to my car to tell me the most nasty, vile thing, thinking it's funny. It's like, "Dude, we're at temple, man!"

It's mostly fine. Adults commiserate with other adults about their lewd fantasies and anecdotes all the time. But it can get out of hand. Michelle remembers one instance in which we went to a dinner with another couple at this really posh, elegant spot. Very expensive.

We're all dressed to the nines. The menus are set down by the server wearing his bow tie and vest and all that traditional garb. As soon as he walks away, the woman we're with says to my wife, "It's true; I like it in the ass."

Come on! We hadn't even ordered *drinks* yet!

Since it's been twenty years of my doing what I do at Mr. Skin, our closer friends and family have gotten used to it to the point that it's not so novel to them anymore. We're just Jim and Michelle, average suburban Chicagoans living in our house with our three kids, attending sporting events, going to the movies, and doing whatever it is everyone else does.

Only, what I do *is* a little skewed from the norm, I guess. As Michelle has noted in the past, I therefore will end up receiving treatment from those around us that is also somewhat skewed from the norm.

Michelle loves to dance, and sometimes we'll be at an event or whatnot, and she'll go and start shaking it up on the dance floor while I hang back to hang out, which is more my thing. As soon as she takes off, nearly all the guys in the room zoom over to me and start talking about their sexual proclivities, ask me questions about the site and, of course, try to stump me on celebrity nudity trivia.

There's hardly ever any escaping it: whether I'm at home with the kids, at synagogue, at the kids' school, or even just relaxing on a date night with Michelle at some intimate bistro, I am Jim McBride *and* I'm Mr. Skin. It's something people seem to really want a piece of, and lucky for me, they're often willing to pay for it through my site.

Now, there *have* been a few knockoff sites over the year. Especially when I first started, there were people trying to home in on my action. But they just didn't have the same brand of detailed information or personal passion or humor we had. It's one of the reasons, frankly, that we were able to survive the dot-com bubble burst of 2000–2001 when there were suddenly all these internet start-ups that went *poof* with the wind.

Other sites didn't have the kind of brand loyalty we boasted, and so they took on a business model that was often based around third-party advertising. That all went *poof* too when the bubble burst—all these companies were suddenly pulling out their stakes and advertising dollars, hightailing it the hell out of Silicon Dodge, with nothing left to bolster the fledgling internet companies that flailed until they flopped.

We survived that cutthroat limbo between Web 1.0 and Web 2.0 because *our* economic strategy is largely based on member subscriptions, not faceless corporations just looking to invest their money for a quick, easy buck without a care about the company or people behind the company or often even the product they're staking.

We didn't worry when advertisers pulled out of internet companies, because guess what? We had enough regular memberships, people who kept wanting to pay for what we were offering them, that we made it through the storm unscathed.

One person who *did* have the knack was this guy named Mike who has the same gift for celebrity nudity that I possess. He was so good, in fact, that I hired him on and he became known as "Skin Jr." in our office.

Mike specialized in foreign films. He was like the Mr. Skin of exotic movies from other lands. This guy can rattle off names and actresses and directors you would probably not even be able to pronounce, let alone fully recall.

I ended up having Mike help out with our content department for a while, because it has always been my goal to make certain our database includes *every single nude scene ever*, which means not only those plucked from English-language flicks and television shows.

This is why, back in the days before streaming and just about everything you could possibly ever want to find residing *somewhere* online, we would use all these special tricks to fill out our archive. Sam had

Two of the Skin Lab's most dynamic pioneers in the science of boob-counting, crack-identifying, and intense pube-detection: Doc (left) and Skin Jr.

eight Netflix accounts and two online Blockbuster accounts (remember *them*?). This way, he could keep his order queues filled to the brim, since they would only allow you to rent out so many movies at a time per individual account. This kept our mailboxes filled with more and more DVDs all the time.

I think Sam had at one time *four* accounts at brick-and-mortar Blockbusters, too!

As we all know, though, some of the hottest, sultriest scenes come from the milieu of foreign flicks. Which is why I sent Sam and Mike to Central and South America to grab some films we couldn't find back up here in the States.

Since Sam had spent some time in Spain, he spoke Spanish fairly well and accompanied Mike to places like Guadalajara, Mexico. They would go to every tiny village you've ever heard of (and a bunch you haven't), seeking out all the video stores they could.

Mike would pull out from the shelves every movie he knew from his Skin Jr. memory bank, and Sam would then drop them in a pile on the counter: "*Tomaremos estos, por favor.*"

Because these were video *rental* stores, the store owners had no idea what these *loco gringos* were up to. But, money talks, so Sam and Mike were able to get all these movies at cost before packaging them up and shipping them off back to the office here in Chicago. All these super-rare titles hardly anyone would be familiar with...except for a guy like Skin Jr.

And don't get me started with all the Asian films Mike filled our shelves with. This guy knew them all!

SKIN JR'S TOP FIVE FAVORITE FOREIGN FLICKS FOR NUDITY

5. *Una Spirale di nebbia* (France)
4. *Room in Rome* (Spain)
3. *Sex and Lucia* (Spain)
2. *La Belle Noiseuse* (France)
1. *Blue Is the Warmest Color* (France)

SKIN JR'S TOP FIVE FAVORITE FOREIGN NUDE SCENES

5. **Maria Valverde**—*Madrid, 1987* (Spain) (0:30)
4. **Laura Antonelli**—*The Divine Nymph* (Italy) (0:14)
3. **Sophie Marceau**—*Beyond the Clouds* (France) (0:49)
2. **Donatella Damiani**—*La liceale seduce I professori* (Italy) (1:16)
1. **Georgina Leeming**—*Virgin* (UK) (S1, Ep4)

Mike did like Fleetwood Mac and went his own way after a while. But I'll never forget going into his office where he'd have piles and piles of all these random movies from all over the world lying around; you'd ask for something extremely obscure, some movie you could hardly even name for the lack of vowels in its title, and he'd know exactly where it was in his orderly chaos.

Skin Jr.'s contributions were just one of many elements of our earlier days that helped broaden our scope and connect with more and more fans. *Buenos tiempos!*

The Voice of Skin

I do want to make a point here that—while I can't speak for Mike—I don't think what we're talking about here with celebrity nudity memorization is necessarily the same thing as having a photographic memory. Some people have said this about me, including Howard Stern. It can even turn into a heated debate with my wife: she thinks I have a photographic memory, and I think I don't.

She'll tell you how someone can give me any arbitrary date from history, and I'll give them a historically important event that occurred on said date. I do read a lot of books on presidents, baseball, and other threads from American history. I'm a curious guy who finds this all very interesting.

Yes, if Michelle were to say we have plans on March 18, I might fire off the notable tidbit that President Grover Cleveland was born on that day in 1837. But a lot of this is just that I'm passionate about American history, just as I am about baseball and, of course, celebrity nudity. So that stuff sticks in my head. For whatever reason.

FIVE GREAT PERIOD PIECE NUDE SCENES

Epics set in previous centuries that feature powdered wigs—and not much else.

5. **Kirsten Dunst**—*Marie Antoinette* (0:22)
4. **Marisa Berenson**—*Barry Lyndon* (1:51)
3. **Uma Thurman**—*Dangerous Liaisons* (1:00)
2. **Elizabeth Berridge**—*Amadeus* (1:07)
1. **Gwyneth Paltrow**—*Shakespeare in Love* (0:53)

One of the people who assisted me in organizing this book was interviewing me about this aspect of my life and arbitrarily chose the name of *Desperate Housewives* alum Teri Hatcher. I immediately told him Hatcher's birth date and place (December 8, 1964, and Sunnyvale, California). I wasn't even sure I was right, but my assistant googled Hatcher on his phone and discovered I was.

I may have an insanely good memory, particularly about things I care deeply about. But I don't believe it's photographic. I'm just a guy who *really* loves this stuff.

And it's not like I don't work on it.

As the face of the company and, more importantly, the *voice* of the company on the radio and elsewhere, I really need to know what I'm talking about. I can't let myself get stumped, or I let down the whole company and brand of Mr. Skin.

That's why I keep thousands of flashcards (or, as I call them, "flesh-cards") around with all the celebrity nudity trivia I can fit on them, kind of like a baseball card. (Or, more to the point, my old index cards we used to messenger bids and my funny notes back at the Merc.)

While I'm writing this, I have a card on my desk that reads on the front VALERIE PERRINE, with her DOB (Sept 3, '43), BIRTHPLACE (Galveston, TX), and some notes in reference to her (former Vegas showgirl, made movie debut in *Slaughterhouse 5* in 1972, played "Eve" in 1978's *Superman*....).

On the back of the card, it lays out what movies she was naked in (she shows her breasts in *Slaughterhouse 5* and the black-and-white Lenny Bruce biopic *Lenny* with Dustin Hoffman, in which she plays Bruce's stripper wife; she shows her buns in 1972's *Steam Bath*). Of course, I also always include the time codes in which the nudity takes place, as well.

I keep these cards on my desk in my office, at home by my easy chair, and in various other convenient places where I can pull them out and quiz myself with them periodically while I watch TV or do something else, the same way a lot of people might multitask by watching TV and futzing around on their phone.

It's a hobby of mine, my fleshcards. It's the same as how, back in my studio apartment days, I would keep file cabinets filled with celebrity nudity trivia while I photocopied stills and digitized clips from films and TV. So, you see? It's not solely about having a good memory: it's

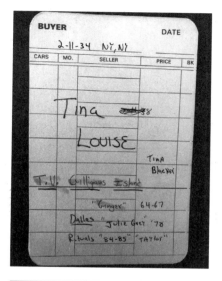
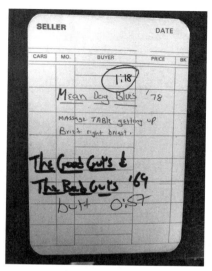
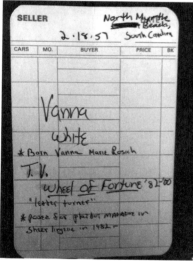
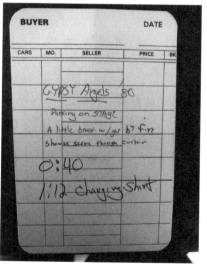

A handful of my "fleshcards." These are actually old Chicago Mercantile Exchange trading cards onto which I would write down nude scene and actress skinfo, years before I had any idea I'd be Mr. Skin. Eventually, I had thousands of these things built up and alphabetized and I would constantly use them to quiz myself like a kid with actual flash cards. The end result has been way more fun than a spelling bee, though!

also about the amount of time and work I put into knowing this stuff like I'm eternally boning up for some final exam to come.

Everyone at Mr. Skin is as hardworking, dedicated, and knowledgeable when it comes to their jobs and departments as I am. Exhibit A is that trusty production manager of mine, Christian, who will work with my production technician Brock in coming up with fresh, innovative concepts for original content like our annual "12 Days of Titsmas" videos.

These are seasonal promotions that we do parodying the traditional Christmas carol, Mr. Skin style. You can just imagine what Christian and Brock can come up with in visualizing "eight maids a milkin'" in a sexy, tongue-in-cheek Mr. Skin tone.

Sam first came up with the idea a few years back. So, he still oversees Christian and Brock storyboarding how the video will ultimately look, what the general outline will be, and how the script contributed by our editorial department—itself overseen by managing editor Vera—will be incorporated into the final product. As with so much we do at Mr. Skin, it's a truly collaborative effort.

"It's basically all these building blocks we put together when we work on a project like this," Christian explains. "And there's a lot of back and forth between everyone before we get to the final product."

"12 Days of Titsmas" is such an all-hands-on-deck affair, in fact, that we'll often tap the vocal talent of my office administrator Lisa to add the singing. Though I'm the one who usually does all the voiceover for videos—hey, I'm Mr. Skin, and I'm the one on the radio for hours a day, years on end!—*Lisa* is the one with the master's degree in opera performance.

"Yeah," Lisa says, "they said, oh, you're a singer, so you can sing all these naughty songs for us! And I agreed, because...I guess I'm just like that!

It's the script, though, that is really the foundation of what we're doing with these promotional videos and other original content. A well-crafted script is so essential to help guide the process and all the folks in design and tech who need to know exactly what to do.

As the ones composing these scripts, it's Vera's and the editorial department's responsibility to make sure these specialty products are not only lively and entertaining, but also *consistent* with the "Mr. Skin voice." (My former head writer Mike McPadden wanted me to make it clear that he was a principle factor in developing the voice of the site with me. Hold on, McPadden. We're getting to you soon, I swear.)

Here now is the actual writer's style guide for our team at Mr. Skin:

MR. SKIN EDITORIAL GUIDELINES

In plain terms: how to write for MrSkin.com.

1. HUMOR

Right away, let us stress the key ingredient that must inform any and all aspects of MrSkin.com:

Humor is Priority One

If you are ever struggling with an idea or at a loss for how to complete a piece, refer back to the above statement—every time. Site visitors must always be amused and amazed by our funny turns of phrase and creative employment of language. Among the tools:

Invented words

"Furburgerage" (meaning "pubic hair") has become Mr. Skin's signature term. The site describes the largest-size breasts as "Jamambo!" Follow those leads. Use "skin" as a prefix or suffix whenever possible; e.g.—"skinpire," "skintastic," etc. Meld "mam," "muff," and other such existing slang terms into larger compounds. Another great suffix: "shish," as in "gashish." Go wild and have fun. If a word makes you laugh out loud when you think of it, submit it immediately.

Puns

The punnier, the funnier. No pun is too "dumb" or too obvious to consider. All puns, however, should refer to nudity, body parts and/or sexuality. "Crack" and "meat" alone are gold mines.

Alliteration

Sexy starlets sumptuously sizzle showing skin on the site. Our writers romp righteously by wrangling rapturous word-plays as well.

Rhyming couplets

The site's definition of ménage a trois is "gleesome three-somes." A nice term for butt is "seat meat." Do it to it.

Brevity

The soul of wit. 'Nuff said!

2. TONE

MrSkin.com is light, fun, vibrant, bouncy, and retro. Think of a '50s cocktail party. Look to the Mr. Skin logo for guidance. Design-wise, the site has a "Nick at Nite" feel that must be reflected in the editorial. However, we must also communicate sexiness. Focus on these concepts when writing:

- Bawdy
- Naughty
- Randy
- Ribald
- Burlesque
- Raised-eyebrow
- Elbow-to-the-ribs
- "Wink-wink, nudge-nudge"

MrSkin.com's content is R-rated, but the language should largely be kept PG-13. Avoid harsh words and obscenities (fuck, cunt, cock, pussy, blowjob, etc.), except when their impact is nullified by a particularly strong joke. Examples: a nude woman in a karate fight is deemed "cunt fu fighting;" monsters who have sex with humans are described as "fuckin' freaks."

A light touch is especially important in describing hard-edged material. Impress us with your creative subtlety.

3. ATTITUDE

Always be positive and upbeat. Always. MrSkin.com is a fan site. Every celebrity profile should be written directly for a fan who is in love with that given celebrity. Each movie review should speak directly to a fanatical devotee of that movie.

Someone's attractiveness is not the writer's call to make. The guy looking up Kathy Bates or Jessica Tandy (who, at age 84, was nude in 1994's Camilla) is actively seeking to see those women naked. We are on his side. He must not be insulted.

Again: MrSkin.com is a party and we're celebrating famous women getting naked. Kathy Bates and Jessica Tandy, therefore, are to be congratulated, as is the guy who is looking for them.

There is also legal motivation to keep our language full of praise: negative words could lead to negative attention.

Occasions will arise when we may joke at a celebrity's expense—e.g., the Top Ten Actresses I Wish Kept Their Clothes On—but these are rare exceptions and will be dealt on an individual basis.

4. POINT OF VIEW

All material comes from "Mr. Skin." There are no bylines. The general idea is that Mr. Skin—that guy whose face serves as our logo—is situated in his nudity-strewn basement, giddily and perpetually digging up new material to share with site members.

Conjure the feel of direct communication, but go easy on using "I," "we," and "our." Let the site speak for itself, as though personally addressing the visitor as he looks over Mr. Skin's shoulder.

In order to help maintain this consistency (so that people will know when they're watching, listening, or reading that it's absolutely a Mr. Skin production), Vera is also the one who is in charge of finding and hiring our writers who will fit with our style.

She's mostly seeking out a specific "personality" in the potential hires, like-minded cohorts who will gracefully transition into our cozy clubhouse here at Mr. Skin.

Like a lot of media outlets these days, it's not about whether someone went to journalism school necessarily. An ideal candidate might not have gone to college at all. It's really about the kinds of writing samples they provide and whether they can write in the voice of Mr. Skin.

Can the candidate be funny? Are they an expert at "Dad jokes" and puns, especially? That's the Mr. Skin way, after all, so Vera needs to make sure these potential hires are not only good writers, but writers who can produce in our style.

That "very 1950s or 1970s cocktail party" style, as Vera elaborates: "It's like you're in a sunken living room, everyone is having cocktails, and somebody jumps in the pool and goes skinny-dipping. That vibe of everyone's having fun, getting naked, celebrating it, with a lot of jokes being made. No one's taking anything too seriously. Nothing's ever life or death; just, 'Oh, this is a fun time!' That's the Mr. Skin voice I'm looking for in writing samples."

Our design team and folks like our creative director Dan don't have a concrete style guide of their own, which means a lot of what they concoct is guided by an unspoken sense of what works, what the audience wants, and what else is on the market.

It's about "feeling it out" for them, when it comes to the visual design of what we do with Dan and his guys, especially since—again—we *all* work so closely together, watching over one another as appropriate to stay on the same page when it comes to the Mr. Skin look and voice (even if we can't all articulate it quite as specifically as Vera!).

Minding the Store

How involved do I get in these specialty projects? I'll let Christian answer that one:

"Skin's not necessarily breathing down our necks or anything. He's sort of more like an overall curator of the site and its content in general. We already sort of know what he's going to want when we're working on these projects, because we've all been working for him for so long now."

I know my guys are good at what they do, and I make sure to pop in when I can to help them cut stuff out or add stuff in or, in the case of something like "12 Days of Titsmas," maybe have them swap out certain scenes or actresses featured for others: "Yeah, that's not working. Scrap this. Add that. Take out Angelina Jolie...."

A project like "12 Days of Titsmas" can take three or four weeks to produce, from start to finish. It's a lot of man-hours, and because we don't exactly have a staff the size of Pixar's or DreamWorks', such a project can typically fall on the shoulders of only a few people at a time...who are also multitasking, because they have to keep up their regular work running and adding to the site, as well.

That's another one of the secrets of how we're able to remain so successful, actually. I might be Mr. Skin, but my employees—just as passionate as I am about this stuff—work with me to make Mr. Skin as a company and website *the* place for celebrity nudity online. And our fans know this. As I said before, it's not just that they trust me as the face and voice of Mr. Skin, but they trust *us*, the entire company and site, as a one-stop shop for what they're looking for.

We really are like an expert curatorial service. It's like something a friend of mine at HBO has suggested is the reason cable TV can still survive in the age of online media and streaming services. People know HBO. They trust HBO. HBO has won all these prestigious awards over the years.

When viewers get home, exhausted after a long day's work, they can collapse into their couch, flip on the TV or their computer, and watch what they know will most likely be some pretty killer movies and TV shows, curated (and, so often these days, produced) by the fine folks at HBO.

It's a service, like with Mr. Skin, that they're willing to pay for: not having to seek out the good stuff for hours on end themselves. Don't these viewers have to make enough decisions all day long anyway?

As Sam describes it, we realized early on that we had to go from being more of a "warehouse" of celebrity nudity to being more of a "museum" of celebrity nudity. We don't want people wandering hopelessly around an endless warehouse cluttered with disorganized and misplaced crap, totally lost. We want to give them a meticulously crafted guided experience, kind of like the way I used to go through my cable guide as a kid seeking out the movies with the letter "N" next to their titles.

Think of what happens when someone asks you where you want to go out for dinner. It's easy to pull a blank, especially at the end of the day when you're totally burned out. *What am I hungry for? How much do I want to spend tonight? How far away are these places? What's the weather like outside right now?*

At Mr. Skin, we want to be more like TripAdvisor, more like the well-curated museum, pointing out and detailing what to check out, the stuff you'll likely really dig and that suits your own personal interests. Since, like HBO, we have so many years of proven expertise under our belts, since our branding is so robust, people will trust that they'll have a good experience at our site.

It's why my Skinterns in my content department work their balls off eight hours or more a day scanning through every single movie, TV show, and mobile/online/streaming series that's available, pulling clips and stills, and tagging everything for proper organization. Nothing escapes their eyes!

You can find whatever you want these days online, but we're the ones here to help you decide what to look for when it comes to celebrity nudity. The same reason people are happy to pay for services such as Spotify is the same reason people are cool paying for us.

In the same throbbing vein of Spotify, we pound *hard* on our own playlists to give a shortcut to our users of what's hot and what's not. It can be grueling at times.

Anyone at the office, even our designer Doc, can come up with these lists of themed celebrity nudity lists. He finds them so fun, he'll even put some together off-hours at home if a wacky idea pops him in the brain while he's watching TV or eating a ham sandwich.

He came up with the notion of doing a playlist based on "Girls Named Kate"…but it just didn't pan out. There was another that popped up, but then quickly fell because he just couldn't come up with enough for a playlist themed around Groundhog's Day.

It helps when we align these playlists around special events going on in real life at the time. You remember when *Family Guy* creator Seth MacFarlane hosted the Oscars and notoriously belted out the controversial song "We Saw Your Boobs"? Well, you better believe Doc went right off and found the best boob scenes for each of the actresses MacFarlane named in the song and had an apropos playlist up on MrSkin. com lickety-split.

(I'm gonna say it here: Even though MacFarlane never called us out directly in the song or his many interviews that took place thereafter about it, I'm *fairly* certain he did use our site for research; in fact, as recently as last year, he name-checked us in an episode of his cartoon when main character Peter and son Chris Griffin cry out together to a hologram of a Silicon Valley mogul: "Do you know Mr. Skin?")

Whenever we feel we've shot our load, we fill back up by watching more and more nude scenes. We watch all the *craziest* crap that might otherwise fly by your radar, or not even make a blip on your screen at all. We *love* promoting movies and shows that get little to no attention elsewhere.

Like this insane film from a few years ago called *Assholes*. I swear to you, that's its title. Really wild low-budg film that billed itself as "one of the grossest films of all time." A whole new level of filth that would make John Waters himself toss his cookies.

The director of *Assholes*, Peter Vack, jammed in all this wild hardcore nudity involving ass-eating and what we call a teeter-totter (you can check out what the heck that is on our site!). It's all this stuff that even a guy like me would never conceive of before...and meanwhile the star of the film is Peter's own sister—whose name is Betsey Brown (go figure). Vack even slipped in cameos by his parents. What a visionary!

Hardly anyone would ever think to seek out a movie like *Assholes*, but we go through material like this all the time. We want to make sure we see *everything*, no matter how obscure, strange, or disgusting.

"Some of the stuff we watch," Doc says, "you need a shower for your mind afterwards!"

BROWN GOLD: THE RAREST OF ALL CELEBRITY NUDITY—CELEBRITY BUTTHOLE

When it comes to female nudity, "T&A" are the two most prominent letters of the alphabet, as well as a reference to the most frequently flaunted naked lady parts on film.

Less often unveiled but not entirely infrequent would be the lower frontal, feline-nicknamed female anatomical area that might turn the aforementioned phrase into the acronym "T.A.P."

Then there is the most private of all private parts; the backdoor byway that in an all-points-exposed nude scene would invite the abbreviation "T.A.B."—yes, the celebrity butthole.

In twenty years of professionally anal-lyzing fleshy revelations on film, I've come across only a scant gland-ful of brave starlets who have dared to bare tush-tunnel and, every time, it's a cause for rect-acular celebration (aren't you glad I didn't write "smell-ebration"?).

- **Sherilyn Fenn**—*Two Moon Junction*. (1:24) Forget *Twin Peaks*—here's Sherilyn between the cheeks! In the greatest celebrity butthole scene of all time, Sherilyn bares all and mounts a muscular male carnie, arching her back to show off her sumptuous keister-crater.

- **Holly Hunter**—*The Piano*. (1:03) While preparing a bed on which to bang Harvey Keitel, completely nude Holly turns her back to the camera and bends forward to reveal both hairy back-burger and a nifty glimpse of her Academy-Award-winning heinie hollow.

- **Helen Shaver**—*The Believers*. (1:17) Helen hops out of bed in her birthday suit, grants us a peek at her posterior portal, as well as a scruff of back-muff that mouth-wateringly proves she doesn't adhere to her own last name.

Or how about *this* scene, courtesy of our office administrator Lisa:

"I must have been here for about three or four months, so still pretty new to the company. I was tagging clips, and on my computer screen is a man and a woman naked in a bathtub. And they're both playing trumpets. They're playing the '1812 Overture' on trumpets. Naked in the bathtub together. I'm tagging the scene, thinking, 'This is hilarious!' I kind of sense someone behind me, and it's Skin. He sees what's on my screen, and I turn around and he and I make eye contact.

"He's got this great shit-eating grin on his face. It was like he was telegraphing, 'I created this moment. I created this workplace. This is what my day is and now what her day is, too!' It was a moment of joy and amusement, all wrapped up into one. That scene—both from the movie and real life of our both watching the scene from the movie—will always stick with me. Where else would you work where you'd see that kind of thing? Naked people in a bathtub playing trumpets. I didn't even know that existed before, but now I do!"

That's right: Mr. Skin—the one office where you're doing something wrong if you *don't* have something NSFW on your screen!

(PS: The 2007 movie Lisa was watching is called *Hannah Takes the Stairs*. That's Greta Gerwig playing dueling trumpets topless. It's sure to give you your own trouser trombone.)

The Devil in the Details

As of 2018, we were tracking 137 shows across thirty-five networks of television. And that's just TV. Imagine all the movies, supplemented by an endless litany of web series and exclusive mobile series.

BOOB TUBE BESTS: FIVE MOST SKINTASTIC TV SHOWS FOR NUDITY

TV series that lasted five seasons or more that had us reaching for more than just the remote.

5. *Dream On*
4. *True Blood*
3. *Californication*
2. *Shameless*
1. *Game of Thrones*

We delight in being able to shine some light on content, like this talk show Sarah Silverman had on Hulu. A talk show...with *nudity*? Where do you ever get to see *that*? It was pretty cool: Sarah—a big fan of Mr. Skin, by the way—had two naked people in her audience, so of course we had to make sure all of our Skin fans could see it. Because, really, how many people are going to think they'll find nudity hidden away in a talk show on Hulu?

A while back, we featured clips from an Amazon pilot episode of a comedy…that never ended up going to series. That's how extensive our search will get: we'll show you material from shows that never even get made! In this case, the pilot for the show—*Salem Rogers*—featured the nude debut of the beautiful Leslie Bibb modeling on a catwalk bare-ass naked in front of an appreciative crowd. The scene doesn't end well for her—she gets tasered—but we couldn't leave that shockingly great scene off our site. Even though the series never made it to production.

We even featured a quick moment from a livestream of Katy Perry that was on for a limited time only. There's a brief few seconds when, while Perry's getting a full-body massage, we're granted a lovely shot of the "I Kissed a Girl" crooner's butt. We made sure to grab and tag it for our members: a very Perry cheek peek!

SKIN SCORES: THE RAREST NUDE SCENES DISCOVERED TO DATE

Ultra-obscure T&A treasures unearthed by Mr. Skin's crack archeologists.

As Mr. Skin, I'm not just the world's foremost authority on naked celebrities, I'm also out to hunt down and share every single movie and TV nude scene ever made.

Knowing about a super-rare instance of an actress going bare is one thing; showing it is what truly puts MrSkin.com in a class by itself.

So, while, of course, the site features pics and clips of Sharon Stone in *Basic Instinct* and Angelina Jolie in, well, a lot of movies, here are a few buried treasures I really had to do some digging to be able to showcase.

- **Victoria Principal**—*The Naked Ape*
  Playboy magazine's sole foray into movie production was *The Naked Ape*, a big screen adaptation of a popular treatise on human sexuality by hip anthropologist Desmon Morris. While the movie has slipped through the cracks, it will live forever as the best naked vehicle for Dallas TV star Victoria Principal, who bares her own Big D's twice here.

- **Melanie Griffith**—*Ha-Gan*
  Nineteen-year-old Melanie is nude in this otherwise entirely forgotten Israeli drama about an urban garden. Melanie shows exactly how her own garden grows, going full frontal and appearing naked in three separate scenes.
- **Marta Kristen**—*Gemini Affair*
  Kristen (who played Judy Robinson on Lost in Space) has a skin-tastic lesbo scene with Kathy Kersh at the 0:57 minute mark. Danger, Will Robinson!

HOLE-Y GRAILS

Legendary nude scenes still eluding Mr. Skin's one-armed grasp.

For Hollywood comedy fanatics, Jerry Lewis's *The Day the Clown Cried* is an object of fascination, frustration, and, ultimately, inspiration. The funnyman's never-released WWII concentration camp farce is said to be locked in a private vault and has only ever been seen by a precious few who came away awestruck by its sheer...Jerry-ness.

In Mr. Skin terms, a few movies' nude scenes are rumored to exist that even my crack staff and I have never been able to track down... yet. These following buried T&A treasures comprise my personal *The Day the Clown Cried*.

If these uni-horn/snatch-squatch/Loch-Breast-Monster-like scenes really are bare and really are out there, I'll find them...or at least cry trying!

- **Jean Simmons**—*Spartacus*
  Jean Simmons' skinny-dip scene in Stanley Kubrick's ancient Rome epic was scandalous enough to make audiences at the time believe they saw her bare all. It's close, but you don't get to actually see 'em in (or out) of the Colosseum. Rumor has it, though, that Kubrick did shoot nude footage of Jean's beans and I'm on a hero's quest to track it down. I am Hard-icus!
- **Claire Bloom**—*80,000 Suspects*
  The British pandemic thriller *80,000 Suspects* features two suspects I'm on the hunt for—Claire Bloom's naked chest-buds! Claire was a darling of England's acting elites, as Charlie Chaplin, Laurence Olivier, and Richard Burton all sought her out as a co-star. Since then, I've been seeking out Claire's rosy, exposed rack which supposedly was filmed in full, then lost. Nip, nip, cheerio!

> • **Claire Bloom and Jennie Linden**—*A Severed Head*
> In *A Severed Head*, Claire bares again, allegedly, alongside robust redhead Jennie Linden. While I'm out looking to get some *Head*, be sure to check out Jennie's juggables in the Ken Russell skin classic, *Women in Love*.

My content department is filled with eight full-time Skinployees sitting dedicated at their computer screens, going through movie after movie, show after show, each and all day. They're seeking out cheek peeks, as well as nip slips, weird fetishes, and unique elements of scenes throughout each asset of content they go through.

This is how, when you're watching a clip on our site and see a tag for "tight bike shorts" from said scene, you can say to yourself, "Hey, I like that! I want to see more!" You click on the tag, and you've suddenly got a whole mess of other clips from other movies and shows that will give you all the "tight bike shorts" shots your little heart desires.

Can the work get overwhelming? Well, with so much stuff constantly coming through the pipeline, one of my Skinterns described it in the words of Newman from *Seinfeld*: "The mail never stops!"

The people in my content department are viewing and tagging material so much, in fact, that some of them have admitted to automatically "tagging" scenes from their own lives after they leave the office for the day. It's like they're seeing the world through the augmented-reality-enhanced eyes of the Terminator or RoboCop.

Lisa experienced such a side effect back when she was helping with tagging clips: "Your brain really starts to work like that. I saw a dude getting out of a car, and my brain immediately went, 'Bike shorts, blue bike, summer day….' All these possible 'tags' for the scene so someone could find it at MrSkin.com if they were looking for it. It was not a TV or movie. It was my life! You do start getting sucked in like that. It can be entertaining."

Even our young content manager Joey, who runs the division, has experienced this startling phenomenon: "Yeah, the work can get so repetitive that you start seeing people on the subway or something and start tagging things about them. It can be weird. I remember thinking at one point, 'I gotta curb this.'"

It can also be daunting for my guys in content sometimes because of how seriously we need to take the details of each scene and tag. Everything must be 100 percent accurate, as you know. *We're* the sexperts, and we can't be wrong, or our credibility can go right down the toilet.

Here's the kind of conversation we'll have at the office that illustrates how seriously we take the accuracy of the information we provide for each clip. This was taken from a recording for one of our Anatomy Awards meetings that involved one of our content guys, Be, our managing editor Vera, and a few other folks from around the company. We were watching clips and stills projected on the wall, courtesy of Joey's own special app he developed to do just that:

JOEY: *Okay, "Best Breast"...*

SKIN: *Wait, quick question: Does anyone looking at those think they might be fake?*

BE: *No.*

SKIN: *My concern is, they're so perfect, I think they might be fake.*

VERA: *They're too small to be fake.*

SKIN: *Well, no. There are a lot of women who have A-cup breasts that go to Bs or Cs. I just want to make sure. We do have a video of her...I just want to make certain.* [Joey runs the clip in full] *Yeah, the full video helps, because we can see her moving around.* [the clip continues] *Eh, those aren't real.*

VERA: *They're real.*

SKIN: *No, they're fake.*

VERA: *Oh, I was looking at the other breasts in the shot!*

BE: *That girl won "Best Ass Flash" last year.*

Or how about something as seemingly simple as which name we should use when referencing an actress? Here's another excerpt from a later conversation we had in the same meeting:

BE: *I think the name listed there is a fake name.*

SKIN: *Is that what she's credited by in the movie?*

BE: *It's not her real name. I don't think we should use it.*

SKIN: *So, it's a fake name? Does she use it?*

BE: *I mean…It's the name she's going by.*

SKIN: *Look, if it's her stage name, that's the name we should use.*

VERA: *Her boyfriend goes by "Rusty Nails."*

And speaking of fakery, what about merkins? Merkins are the bane of my existence. They really are. With more and more girls wearing them in full-frontal scenes these days, it makes our job even tougher when it comes to accuracy. The fake versus real breasts quandary is something that can be looked up: you can find out if some girl has breast implants or not and when she got them. But whether a girl is wearing a merkin can make determining what's real and what's not down below almost impossible sometimes.

I mean, can we honestly say it's "full-frontal" if we're not sure if the girl is wearing a merkin? Think about it for a second: If she *is* wearing a merkin, she might as well be wearing a bikini bottom, and therefore it's *not* really a "full-frontal" moment, is it?

THAT'S A MERKIN! FIVE TIMES WE KNOW FAKE PUBES WERE USED

As full-grown muff fluff has fallen out of favor among actresses, many shaved starlets sneakily slip on pubic wigs—aka merkins—to simulate hair-down-there.

5. **Kate Winslet**—*The Reader* (0:20)
4. **Patricia Arquette**—*Human Nature* (1:19)
3. **Bottomless Party Girls**—*Harold & Kumar Escape from Guantanamo Bay* (0:26)
2. **Christina Ricci**—*Z: The Beginning of Everything* (S1, E4)
1. **Olivia Wilde**—*Vinyl* (S1, E6)

Fake *anything* can be troublesome for us. Which is why we'll often draw together the power of the entire office when we're trying to figure out whether a certain body part is genuine or not.

THE ☆ STRIP

"ATTACK OF THE MERKINS!"

SIMPLY PUT, A MERKIN IS A PUBIC WIG THAT A WOMAN CAN WEAR OVER HER VAGINA TO GIVE HER THE APPEARANCE OF HAVING A BUSHIER BUSH (OR ONE AT ALL).

A MERKIN CAN BE VERY USE-FUL FOR ACTRESSES & FILM-MAKERS WHO WISH TO GIVE THEIR CHARACTER THE LOOK OF BEING "PERIOD"...

(NO, NOT THAT PERIOD!)

SQUIRT!

...IF THE MOVIE OR TV SHOW IN WHICH THE CHARACTER EXISTS IS FROM AN EARLIER TIME...

BACK WHEN MANY WOMEN DID NOT SHAVE OR GROOM THEIR PUBIC HAIR.

SHOWING OR NOT SHOWING PUBIC HAIR CAN ALSO SIGNIFIC-ANTLY AFFECT A FILM'S RATING (AND THEREFORE COMMERCIAL PROJECTIONS)...

WHICH IS ANOTHER REASON MERKINS ARE SOMETIMES EMPLOYED IN FILMS OR TV SHOWS.

MERKINS MAY HAVE BEEN USED AS EARLY AS THE 1200s!

BEING MEMBERS OF THE SO-CALLED "EARLIEST VOCATION", PROSTIT-UTES WERE LONG IN THE HABIT OF SHAVING THEIR PUBIC HAIR FOR SANITARY PURPOSES...

AND THEN, BECAUSE THE WAXED LOOK WAS NOT A TRENDY STYLE AT THE TIME, WOULD GET A MERKIN MADE...

AND WEAR THEM IN ORDER TO APPEAR MORE ALLURING TO THEIR CUSTOMERS.

ADDITIONALLY, MEN PLAYING WOMEN IN THEATER SHOWS BACK IN THOSE EARLIEST DAYS, WOULD WEAR MERKINS IN ORDER TO COVER UP THEIR PENISES AND APPEAR — WELL — LIKE THEIR WOMEN CHARACTERS.

SPECULATION IS ALL WE HAVE TO UNDERSTAND THE DERIVATION OF THE TERM "MERKIN" ITSELF.

ACCORDING TO THE OXFORD ENGLISH DICTIONARY, IT'S POSSIBLE "MERKIN" CAME FROM THE WORD "MALKIN," A NICKNAME FOR THE WORDS "MAUDE" & "MARY," COMMON NAMES FOR LOWER CLASS WOMEN BACK IN THE DAY.

MERKINS FOR DUMMIES

MERKINS WERE PARTICULARLY POPULAR BETWEEN THE 1600s-1800s...

AND EVEN FEMALE MEMBERS OF THE ARISTOCRACY WORE THEM, GOING SO FAR AS EMBELLISHING THEM WITH VARIOUS ACCOUTREMENT. EVERYTHING FROM JEWELRY TO FLOWERS.

IN CONCLUSION, NOW YOU UNDERSTAND THE TRUE COMIC GENIUS OF DIRECTOR STANLEY KUBRICK & WRITER TERRY SOUTHERN IN WHOSE FILM "DR. STRANGELOVE" THE PRESIDENT OF THE USA IS NAMED "MERKIN MUFFLEY."

Here's an excerpt (edited for clarity) from an hour-long thread plucked from an internal chat service we use throughout the office called Slack. The question on the digital table: whether testicles lain bare in a certain scene are actual balls or a prosthetic "pouch" courtesy of some movie magic:

ERIC [content technician]: *Debating whether this is "balls" or "pouch." Seems a bit large. Any input would be appreciated.* [blurry shot attached].

DOC: *Ha...Going on the side of balls. A tad of taint sold me.*

VERA: *I'd need to see a full clip to judge. For science.*

[full clip uploaded by Eric]

SIMPLE POLL:

REAL (4)

POUCH (7)

VERA: *Everyone, please join the poll.*

STEVE: *Zoom in. You can see the glorious pubes adorning that sac.*

DOC: *Just not enough for me to say "real balls."*

MARILU [content technician]: *I feel like it's suspiciously too many pubes. Looks furry instead of pube-y.*

MATT [photo editor]: *I'm switching my vote to pouch. I'm just not certain beyond a reasonable doubt, your honor.*

BE: *I say call it real till proven otherwise!*

STEVE: *Seems awfully wasteful for an indie film to spend money hand-stitching a fake ball sac for some guy that's like got a hairy-as-hell sac. He looks like Glen Hansard to me, and when I think Glen Hansard, I think, "That guy's got hairy balls."*

JOEY: *Oh, but this was on Amazon. Their budget for fake ball sacs alone is likely in the five-figure range.*

DOC: *Ha.*

STEVE: *Can't give us another season of Jean-Claude Van Johnson, but "Let's stitch up a fake sac."*

SKIN: *Me, Sam, and Christian are getting a kick out of this, but don't have a consensus on balls or not.*

JOEY: *Christian has a veteran's eye. His silence on the matter is disappointing.*

STEVE: *I believe we're sending him to the annual "Is This A Ball Sac Or Not" convention.*

JESSE: *When I think it's close, I side with Doc. He is a ball-spotting expert.*

CHRISTIAN: *Hard to say, but one pic looks like danglers.*

ERIC: *Thanks for the input, everyone! Seems like the "pouch"s have it. The end.*

ANIMAL HOUSE & ARTIFICIAL FUNBAGS

The First Set of Fake Boobs I Ever Saw—And Didn't Know It!

To love movies in general, and movie nudity in particular, is to be forever awestruck by the 1978 comedy masterpiece, *Animal House*. The taboo-blasting blockbuster broke all manner of ground in terms of how far Hollywood humor could go and how much raunch audiences would come to demand between laughs during R-rated farces.

Animal House also pioneered another area that almost no one is aware of: breast implants on the big screen—and in one of the most iconic nude scenes in movie history, to boot!

At the thirty-nine-minute mark, John Belushi, as head animal Bluto Blutarski, mounts a ladder alongside a nearby sorority and spies into the window of actress Mary Louise Weller as snooty cheerleader Mandy Pepperidge. While Belushi ogles her, Mary Louise peels down to her panties and reveals her perfectly perky naked pair up top.

The reason Mandy Pepperidge's mammaries appear so peppy, though, is because Mary Louise Weller had breast implants—an absolute rarity back then in 1978 and a fact I only learned in 2006 when MrSkin.com ran a Skinterview with *Animal House* co-writer Chris Miller in 2006.

In that Q&A on T&A, Miller told us:

"Mary Louise Weller was a piece of work. She had had some sort of '70s boob job. Have you noticed in the movie? They don't move when she moves! Don't mean to spoil things for anyone, but these were titties o' plastic! Anyway, [Executive Producer] Matty Simmons declared that, in deference to the young lady's nudity, no one but the absolute minimum crew would be allowed on the set. The rest of us, who'd gotten used to hanging around with [Director John] Landis to watch the thing go down, were barred. Of course, Matty made an exception for himself and observed the entire thing. They needed a mature man on the set, in case anything went wrong, he felt."

Skin Gets Staffed

It might appear to an outsider that this is rather odd behavior. Maybe *very* odd behavior. But, hey, this is the job, and my staff is totally cool with it. Making sure they'll be cool with it is a big part of our hiring process.

Ryan, my director of operations, conducts a lot of the new hire interviews and says he can see whether someone is a "good fit" in their eyes fairly quickly. He's had people during the interview outright say that they're choosing between coming to work for us and taking a job from a company like, oh, Groupon…because their girlfriend or wife or whomever has been steering them toward a more quote-unquote "legitimate" company.

"Which is kind of funny," Ryan says. "We're not a start-up anymore. We've been around twenty years. We're established. I'd say that's pretty legitimate."

Sam does a lot of the hiring with Ryan, and for him, it's all about the candidate's chops. If you're applying to be a web developer, he wants to make sure you're an *excellent* web developer. If you're applying to be a graphic designer, you have to have impeccable design skills.

But, yes, Sam is also looking for a certain passion the candidate has for our content. He says this is a "close second" as far as his priorities in looking for a good hire. As strict as Sam can be about finding the most skillful designer for the job, he also knows that if you're not into what we do at Mr. Skin, or if you're reluctant about working for a company like ours, you're not going to work well in our office.

Over the years, Sam and Ryan have become uncannily adept at sussing out who will be a right fit for the company and who should take the job at Groupon. Hence why we have such an enviable staff retention rate here, and why people do end up staying for years and not months (which is extremely rare in the media, entertainment, and tech industries).

We've had our share of people over the years who have snuck through the hiring process but just don't work out. That's of course going to happen at any company, especially when you're growing fast and don't always have the time or resources to vet everyone properly. It's why, as Sam puts it, we try our best to "hire slow and fire fast."

We try to be fair, but if it's not working out, we'd rather make the decision to let someone go sooner than later, because there can be a ripple effect throughout the entire office if someone turns out to be a cancer at the company. We're all very dependent on one another, and so we have to work very much in sync, which doesn't happen if someone's dragging their feet or otherwise not into what we're doing.

It has only happened a handful of times, but I *have* fired people who might have been really good at their jobs but also turned out to be total assholes. One guy years back was getting us a ton of new joins every day. But he also ended up being a psycho, literally threatening me at times. It completely freaked me out. He had to go, regardless of how good he may have been at making us a massive amount of money.

As time goes by, you start to say to yourself, "Fuck it: I only want employees who are good people. I don't need the aggravation otherwise."

My favorite story of someone who wasn't right for our little club-house here at the office is about a woman who was *very* uptight. I'm not even sure why she decided to work with us, but there she was, fuming all the time about every minor thing.

At our office in Wicker Park, see, we had two bathrooms. Only two. With nearly fifty people in the office.

We have a lot of young people on staff, and young people like to eat. And drink. A lot. So, there was always a long line going to the bathrooms. You would see the door open, and the person coming out would practically be shoved out of the way by another person running through the door to get there before someone else would take their spot.

It was a...*crappy* situation; I'll give this very uptight woman that.

But it's also something we *all* had to suffer through. Together. Even Sam, Ryan, and me—the people running the company. No one had special privileges.

There were obviously other problems this lady had with the job, but because this was back when I was still more shy about firing people, she was able to stay on as long as she could handle it. When she finally did decide to hit the ol' dusty trail and flee the company, she sent this email that has since become legendary.

It harshly reprimanded whomever was inconsiderate enough not to double flush, effectively leaving behind "poo swirls" in the toilet bowl for her to forever find whenever she went into the bathroom.

We never did solve the Case of the Poo Swirl Culprit. His or her true identity will forever remain a mystery of the ages. But we do still look at that email from time to time and shit our pants laughing.

MrSkin: FWD: To the disrespectful bathroom bandit

Begin forwarded message:

From: "█████████" <██████████████████████>
Subject: MrSkin: To the disrespectful bathroom bandit
Date: July 10, 2007 3:01:30 PM CDT
To: <█████████████████████>

If you are an adult and have successfully made it through elementary school, you should know that you should not exit a bathroom when you have left the toilet bowl covered in poop swirls. So to whoever did this, please find some common sense and respect for those around you and grow up.

████████████
Associate Editor
SK Intertainment
████████████

!DSPAM:4693e5fc3085418781799221 _____
Skinners mailing list
██████████████████████████████████████

128

A Tale of Two Jims

Because our office *is* an unconventional workplace in which we straddle the line between "adult" and "mainstream," another question that often arises for us is, "What will you tell your kids you do when they're old enough to understand?"

My sister Kristina's kids—both still pretty young—know that Mom helps with the hiring and customer service at Uncle Jim's company. (Kristina's husband, incidentally, thinks what we do is just as hilarious as my wife Michelle.)

When Kristina's kids get older, she says, she'll be totally straight with them: "Some people want to look at naked ladies on the internet." It may not be *her* cup of tea necessarily, but she loves what she does and so, in the end, who cares if some people might not approve?

"Uncle Jim" is how Kristina's kids know me. I'm not only Mr. Skin. I'm also Jim McBride, their mother's brother. Yes, I have a crazy job, one that permits me to do a lot of things that most people will never get to do. But, I'm also just an average guy, a family man.

Here's how Michelle breaks down my day:

"Jim gets out of bed, throws on some workout clothes, goes straight to the basement where he has a little office, gets on the radio, and he's immediately talking about, 'Oh, Scarlett Johansson: *Her boobs! Her butt! Her this, her that!*' And then he comes *up* the stairs and makes breakfast for our kids. *That's* the part that's so funny about what he does."

It can be a real tightrope walk. Like Kristina, I of course have to keep certain things from my children until they get older.

Michelle's answer for "What are you going to tell your kids Daddy does for a living?" is always the same: "We're going to tell them…*Mommy's a lawyer!*"

Our take on how to juggle the kids with my atypical occupation has been changing over the years, as Michelle will tell you. She remembers when the kids had their playroom right outside that basement office of mine from where I'd remotely broadcast to whatever radio show I was featured on that morning. Back then, it was more a matter of, "Shhh, Daddy's working!"

As our kids got older, it became more like, "Okay, *you can no longer go in the basement when Daddy's on the radio!*"

If you think *this* clash between my work and domestic life is awkward, imagine what it was like for me when I was conducting a particularly salacious interview on a radio show…while my father-in-law, who was visiting at the time, was standing right behind me…listening in, wearing his tighty-whities.

Our kids are still young enough for them to not *completely* get what it is Daddy's doing all day. But they do comprehend some parts of it. Which is fine. They might hear me on the radio while playing at a friend's house and say to me later, "Oh, Dad! You're so embarrassing!"

Then there was the time they had every right to be embarrassed. At synagogue.

Though we're not religious, I'm *technically* Catholic and my wife is *technically* Jewish. So, yes, we have three Cashews. (Get it? Catholic + Jewish = *Cashew*.) And for tradition's sake, we wanted to give the kids some background in their heritage and decided on raising them (culturally, at least) Jewish. And, you know something? Our rabbi *loves* me. He loves what I do as Mr. Skin. He'll even hit me up for Mr. Skin swag that he distributes to his rabbi friends.

Anyway, our rabbi asks if I'd like to come and speak about my company at an economic club they have there at the temple. It's an informal organization for local Jews to come and discuss business affairs. Simple stuff.

I have a keynote speech I'm preparing to give at the AVN Awards that year and, believing that I could use the congregation as a test audience for my speech, I tell the rabbi I'll do it. (Which is a sentence I'm sure no person has uttered before. Ever.)

I'm giving my speech—all about Mr. Skin—and the economic club is loving it. Meanwhile, my kids are also at the synagogue in another room for that Sunday school class of theirs.

Michelle can take it from here:

"I'm coming to pick up the kids, and normally they'll come out after class all casual or maybe a little groggy, because it's Sunday morning and all. Not this time. The kids are racing out to the car like they're evacuating a fire."

"How was class?" Michelle asks.

"Mom, it was *terrible!*"

Somehow, the speech I was delivering ended up not only playing off of the speakers in the private room where I was meeting with the economic club. Due to some kind of electronic error, it was also blasting through the *entire building.*

Everyone heard me give my AVN keynote speech.

It was fairly quickly cut off, but over what seemed like a lifetime of what was in fact a few horrifying minutes for my preteen kids surrounded by their giggling, blushing friends in their Sunday school class, they had to hear Daddy being introduced as someone who was about to "talk about nudity in film! Welcome him up, everyone!"

Ryan has been saying for a while now that he's going to follow Michelle's and my lead in how to tackle the "kid question." The necessity for this dawned on him one day when he was eating breakfast with his family and got up to leave, grabbing his umbrella emblazoned with a Mr. Skin logo.

His daughter—barely a toddler—pointed at the logo and excitedly proclaimed, "Mr. Skin!"

This *floored* Ryan, who still hasn't the slightest idea how his barely toddler-aged daughter understood that our logo signifies Mr. Skin.

"I took a video of her pointing to the logo on my shirt a little after this," Ryan said, "and she's saying the name of the company over and over again. I posted it on Slack for the whole office to see. Jim came over to my desk and said, 'Wait until you have to answer that question when she starts going to school.'"

Michelle's life has obviously been forever altered by my being Mr. Skin, too. In fact, she was pretty reluctant at first to be considered Mrs. Skin.

For an entire decade, Michelle would be at home listening to me on *Howard Stern,* thinking about how "fucking hilarious" this whole thing was and remaining so fucking glad she wasn't on the show with me.

She was always supportive, but as a nice Jewish attorney girl, it was still something she wanted to stay the hell away from for herself. In talking about what I did to colleagues and acquaintances, she might use euphemisms like "he works for the internet" or "he's in media" or maybe "he has a movie review site." All true assessments, but not very specific.

Then one day, for whatever reason, she realized, "You know what? *Fuck it.*" Why was she being so uptight about what I did for a living? Especially since, you know, the site and company were working. We were a success. It was something to be proud of for me *and* for her.

Plus, she came to figure that she was missing out on all the fun!

"What," she said to herself, "am I going to end up a grandma and will look back on all of this kicking myself that I never went onto *Howard Stern?*"

When the proposal came for her to join me on *Howard Stern* for the tenth anniversary of Mr. Skin, she had a friend who encouraged her, saying, "You go out there and *represent!* He's your man!" And Michelle knew her friend was absolutely right. It was time for her to join the party.

"Howard interviewed me with Jim for his site's tenth anniversary for forty-five minutes," she remembers, "and I almost had a heart attack! It was hysterically funny, because I was also the president of a women's cancer foundation, and then here I am doing *this*, being on *Howard Stern* talking about celebrity nudity!"

"Right after we were done, I had to rush over to a meeting at Morgan Stanley…and had forgotten my blazer I needed, so I could tone down my outfit. You should've seen what I looked like, having come straight from this crazy on-air interview on *Howard Stern* about Mr. Skin, to now being at this totally straitlaced meeting at Morgan Stanley. I had to get serious and down to business, but couldn't stop laughing about what I had just been through."

In case you missed her, here's an excerpt from the forty-five-minute long episode:

HOWARD: Here's Mr. Skin and his attractive wife.

ROBIN: Hi there.

HOWARD: I never thought you could get such a hot wife.

ROBIN: Yeah, look at her.

HOWARD: She's hot.

ROBIN: *She's beautiful.*

HOWARD: *I can't even see her because Garry's blocking her. Wow, you are attractive. When you're an attractive girl obviously you can get, ya know, you can get guys. I mean I'm sure that was not your problem and uh, you could get any guy in here. So when you meet like a guy, did Mr. Skin tell you right away he was Mr. Skin, or how long did he wait to tell ya?*

MRS. SKIN: *He did, I knew he was Mr. Skin. I was sort of going as my girlfriend's wingman.*

HOWARD: *Right.*

MRS. SKIN: *They were hitting on each other and I came to meet him at a party and I said to her before we went there, "If you're going to date Mr. Skin, please let me be there when you tell your father."*

HOWARD: *Right.*

MRS. SKIN: *I need to be the fly on the wall because he'll die.*

HOWARD: *He's an expert, he's, like like like, let's be honest, your husband spends most of his life looking at movies and just like fast-forwarding to the good parts.*

MR. SKIN: *Still does.*

HOWARD: *And it's weird, right?*

MRS. SKIN: *Well I've gotten used to it, ya know?*

HOWARD: *And God bless you guys…*

ROBIN: *Can't you get used to anything? I mean is that what we're seeing here?*

HOWARD: *God blessed you guys with daughters, right?*

MRS. SKIN: *Yeah, two.*

HOWARD: *So it's even harder to explain it to them. Have you explained it to them?*

MRS. SKIN: *No. They stop by the office and they go, "Mommy, look, there's boobies!" On the walls, they're everywhere.*

HOWARD: *How old are the kids?*

MR. SKIN: *Five, three, and almost two.*

ROBIN: *You have three.*

MR. SKIN: *Yeah, three kids. Girl, boy, girl.*

HOWARD: *Let me tell you something. I thought as a dad, ya know, based on what we do, I always thought it wasn't weird what we did. That my daughters would never...*

ROBIN: *Have a problem?*

HOWARD: *Yeah, like wow, three daughters, who would even, ya know. That had to be the most confusing thing, I mean, I was on TV every night spanking chicks and stuff. But, Mr. Skin is like, he's down in his basement somewhere staring at dirty movies and fast-forwarding to the good parts.*

ROBIN: *And the thing is that until the internet, this was just what he did. It wasn't a business.*

ARTIE [co-host]: *It's not even dirty, it's not even dirty movies. He watches regular movies and finds the dirty stuff in it.*

MR. SKIN: *Having a website gave me credibility.*

ROBIN: *That's right.*

MR. SKIN: *In the 80's...*

HOWARD: *You were doing this anyway.*

MR. SKIN: *I was doing it anyway with nothing to promote. I just did it.*

HOWARD: *So, when you met Mr. Skin, was he already famous Mr. Skin, so that...*

MRS. SKIN: *No no no. I have no excuse. I mean seriously. I don't know what this says about me. But no, he hadn't even launched the website. So I started dating him before that.*

HOWARD: *Did you feel weird the first time like you took your shirt off in front of him and stuff like because he's so into boobs and all that stuff?*

MRS. SKIN: *No. I, uh...you know...*

ROBIN: *What kind of rap did he have?*

Mr. and Mrs. Skin make it a decade on *The Howard Stern Show*. Michelle and I cele-brated our tenth anniversary together on the air in August 2009. Initially, Michelle was just listening from the green room, but once Howard heard that Mrs. Skin was nearby, he invited her into the studio and my favorite appearance to date went down. Also, the bigger news: this gorgeous woman really did marry me!

MRS. SKIN: *It was terrible. He would wear these Hawaiian shirts.*

HOWARD: *Most women would probably go, "I met a handsome guy, but it's like he's Mr. Skin, it's so gross!" It had to be a thing to overcome.*

MRS. SKIN: *He's also very funny and he happens to be—I don't want to ruin his rep—a very intelligent guy, and he's...*

HOWARD: *Did he give a...*

MRS. SKIN: *...very sincere*

HOWARD: *Skintelligent!*

MRS. SKIN: *He's skintelligent.*

HOWARD: *You know he's Skintastic. Did you, in other words, did he have a rep where he would go, "Listen, you know this is how I make my living, and believe me, I could give a shit about boobs or anything like that...."*

ROBIN: *It's truly a business decision.*

MRS. SKIN: *He would never say that because it's not true, he totally gives a shit about boobs.*

Later that same day? Michelle throws on some flip-flops, and there we are together pushing three babies in a stroller in Chicago. No one would have ever guessed the two of us had earlier that day been on *Howard Stern* in New York City talking about celebrity boobs and butts.

Actually, that's not quite right: they *did* probably know, because pretty much everyone in my neighborhood knows what I do. And you know what? They think it's awesome, too!

That's our life: switching back and forth between the two worlds. It's a heck of a lot easier to navigate than you'd think, because—just like with our rabbi and neighbors—nearly *everyone* in our lives think what I do is cool.

It wasn't until my kids were in preschool that Michelle started nudging me that I needed to get a new email. I was still using my company email for everything, and she felt filling out the school forms with an email that revealed my being Mr. Skin was not exactly appropriate.

I did get a new personal Gmail address. But it didn't matter at the preschool. Everyone there still somehow found out. Michelle and I went to a parent-teacher conference, and the teacher—a woman, by the way—is talking with us about the usual stuff involving our kids for about fifteen minutes before she suddenly blurts out, "I have to tell you...I'm a really big fan."

Michelle says, "We were hoping no one would know!"

To which the teacher smirks, replying, "Oh, Michelle.... *Everyone* knows!"

"But we changed Jim's email address!"

Didn't matter. Oh, well! That's the life of Mr. and Mrs. Skin (and their kids!) for you.

It Pays to Be Nice

Up until now, you may be wondering, "Hey, Skin, it's nice that your business has made this great life for yourself and your employees…but aren't you pissing off the filmmakers, studios, and networks producing all the stuff you're cataloging on your site?"

Believe it or not: No. Not at all. In the twenty years we've been in business, we've never had a problem. Incredible, isn't it? Or, maybe not.

Truth be told, it wasn't long after we started making a name for ourselves thanks to Howard Stern and Judd Apatow that the studios, networks, independent filmmakers, and everyone else we're promoting became some of our strongest allies. They may not like to talk about it, and I'm not going to name names here, but they do appreciate what we're doing, because we're helping to give them free publicity that goes out to our millions of Mr. Skin users and radio/podcast listeners.

The recognition we bring them even has a direct effect on our own employees. Be's normally not much of a TV watcher, but he got into watching HBO's original series *The Leftovers* because of his fast-forwarding through episodes at work. Now he's a fan of a show he would have never heard of before if he hadn't been seeking out nudity in it for his job.

Dan had never heard of *Game of Thrones*—the books *or* the HBO series—before scanning episodes for breasts when he was still a Skintern. After going through episode after episode, he discovered how cool it all looked and then wanted to slowly binge through the whole series (up to that point) at home.

HBO, Netflix, and all the other networks, studios, and streaming services are also well aware of another secret of our success: we're *celebrating* the shows and movies they're putting out in promoting the nudity they feature.

There is so much negativity out there online that MrSkin.com stands out once more by being *positive* about what it is we're talking about. All the time. We're putting out *tributes* to nudity. It's win-win for *everyone*.

It's a defining principle at Mr. Skin that *there are no bad nude scenes.*

A prime example is how we reviewed a groundbreaking scene from the 2002 film *About Schmidt*. Jack Nicholson is luxuriating in a hot tub, waiting for Kathy Bates to join him, when there she is, crossing the camera and entering the hot tub...fully nude. Now, I know I'm not alone here thinking Bates is awesome. She's an exceptional actress who has been in some of the best movies of all time. Could anyone forget her Academy Award-winning role in *Misery*?

But we can't deny the fact that she's no spring chicken, and she's a hefty lady. It's part of what made her such a remarkably believable character in the role of Annie Wilkes in *Misery*. Big lady. It's a characteristic that comes up in many of the amazing roles she's taken on over the years.

In talking about her full-on nude scene in *About Schmidt*, then, it would have been easy for my editorial staff and I to say something like, "Oh my god! Kathy Bates, get your clothes back on!" But that's not what we're about at Mr. Skin.

I'm of the opinion that there will always be someone out there who will want to see Kathy Bates naked. So, who am I to rain on their parade? Let them enjoy it! And let's resoundingly champion her choice to be so bold and bare in a nude scene we so rarely see onscreen: that of an older, bigger lady. Why not? *Especially* when it's someone as astounding as Bates.

HELEN MIRREN: NAKED IN SIX DIFFERENT DECADES

Born in 1945 and still shockingly sexy and beautiful, British legend of stage and screen Helen Mirren is the all-time champ for long-distance body baring, having peeled to reveal in six different decades.

Between 1969 (how fitting!) and 2010 (as in "perfect 10"!), Helen's shown melons—and often more—in sixteen roles. And that's just so far. Even now, at age seventy-four, fans are still swellin' for Helen and hoping she'll bare all again.

Given Ms. Mirren's sharp smarts, sassy attitude, and superhumanly erotic allure, that prospect does seem tantalizingly possible.

Following her last unclothed turn(-on) before the camera, Helen said she enjoyed the experience and noted, "I think sex and nudity are really two different things...Sometimes nudity is sexy. Sometimes it's not. Sometimes being clothed is more sexy than being nude. I think people tend to get the two mixed up."

Here are Helen Mirren's six most skintastic movies for nudity, spread wide across six delectable decades.

- *Age of Consent*
- *Caligula*
- *The Cook, The Thief, His Wife, and Her Lover*
- *Royal Deceit*
- *The Roman Spring of Mrs. Stone*
- *Love Ranch*

Look, we're not one of these gossip blogs that have their place, but aren't what we do. We don't attack; we don't instigate dog-piling. Avoiding criticism is something that really sets us apart from pretty much everyone else reviewing movies and shows. We barely poke fun at anything, unless it's innocuous, jovial, and in the spirit of good times for all.

This core of lightheartedness at Mr. Skin is exemplified by our innocent-looking, happy-go-lucky 1950s smiley face logo. You know, the one Paul Rudd imitates when he brings up MrSkin.com to Seth Rogen in *Knocked Up*? (Check the cover of this book, if you need a more immediate reference.)

Before I launched the company, one of my original partners suggested that our logo should be a mock-up of a flasher opening his trench coat, showing off his cash and prizes to the audience. I instinctively knew this was the wrong way to go. I wanted the site—even back in the primordial days—to have a kind of Norman Rockwell-esque, gentle, "everyman" sensibility. Nostalgia about a simpler time in our shared history. The kind of visage you can see in vintage commercials or menus from a fifties diner.

I wanted to establish a sense that when users came to our site, they wouldn't feel dirty. It was the same instinct that drove me to go with "Mr. Skin" over "Mr. Naked."

It appears that I was right. Within two weeks of launching, I got a letter from a member who said what we were doing was great. "I don't feel sleazy going to your site," he wrote. "You have nudity from films,

Jim McBride

From: ███████████████████████
Sent: Wednesday, August 18, 1999 10:52 PM
To: █████████████████
Subject: Re: movie clips and pics question

Thanks for the email

I have spent the last few minutes, (who am i kidding...hours!) reviewing your site and i must admit i am very impressed with its content and quality. The information you provide is accurate and informative and i must admit i'm kinda jealous of some of the promo pics you have of many of the stars even tho they are small in size :) I myself have been a collector of celebs for close to 15 years now and i collect both nudes and non nudes. It is wonderful to see a celeb site that doesn't push horrible fakes trying to get people to join and simply presents the facts and solid information. I searched your site pretty hard looking for something bad but was unable to find anything.

The other thing that I love about your site is that it doesn't make you feel dirty when you get there. There is a classiness to it that I can't explain...also it is FUN and I can tell you guys love what you do...

but it's still a fun site. How you're able to do both at the same time is amazing." I saved the email, because this was *exactly* what I was trying to accomplish with MrSkin.com.

There are several people who work for me—even up to my CFO Jim K.—for whom this is a big reason why they're happy to work at Mr. Skin: how playful and lighthearted we are on the site.

"I wouldn't be able to work here if we were doing things that were stupidly offensive," Joey agrees. "I wouldn't want to be on the side of anything gross like that. It wouldn't make me feel good to come into work every day."

Hey, it's probably why you've read so much of a book about a guy like me, isn't it? I'm not perfect by any means. But I'm not a snarky, mean-spirited jerk, and I make sure everything we do at the site is coming from the same good place.

So Much Tech!

Because I can't reiterate enough just how crucial our tech side is to our continued success, I want to wrap up this section of my story by sounding off a little more about how we keep boosting this element of our operation as much as possible (and then some).

When I first started this whole thing back in 1999, all the movies and shows were on tapes. All the pictures and clips we got were from my old Betamax collection or the video rental stores. Grainy, crappy clips and images. It was what I had to work with, and I think we did pretty damn well with the resources available. Clearly, our fans agreed and helped us get over the early hump to become a thriving business.

As more movies and series came out on DVD, I had my team wipe out everything—and I mean *every thing*—we had on the site so we could replace each clip and screenshot with content pulled from this new, innovative format.

About ten years ago, Blu-ray burst onto the scene. It's six times the resolution of a DVD. So, we then had to transfer everything over to *that* format. Had to do it. Had to keep up with the ever-changing times.

Replacing everything with content from Blu-ray discs was not easy. We already had hundreds of thousands of clips and photos online. It was a herculean effort to wipe out our DVD stuff and upload the Blu-ray stuff. But, this is what people expect from Mr. Skin. It's what they're paying for: the best quality. So, it had to be done.

"Out with the old, in with the nude" is our motto. And it helped us to truly flex our muscles when we featured the most significant nude scene in recent movie history in the way it was always meant to be viewed. At six times the resolution, you could finally see, unveiled by higher-grade technology—*yes, oh, yes!*—the money shot behind those luscious, muscular legs of Sharon Stone's in that notorious upskirt shot scene from the scintillating and scandalous *Basic Instinct*.

We never stop upping our game at Mr. Skin. With twenty years of experience in our back pocket, we still treat each day as though it's our first, as though we still have something to prove to the millions of eyes looking at our site each month. I'd like to think it's this attitude that ultimately answers the question more than any other of how and why we survive and flourish.

I'm so excited to see where we'll go from here in 2020 and the years ahead.

THE★STRIP

"WHY BLU-RAY WAS BETTER"

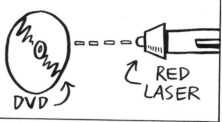

THE NAME "BLU-RAY" DERIVES FROM THE BASIC NOTION THAT WHEREAS DVDs ARE ACCESSED ON PLAYERS VIA A LONGER-WAVELENGTH RED LASER...

DVD

RED LASER

BLU-RAY DISCS (CAPABLE OF CONTAINING DENSER HOURS UPON HOURS OF HIGH-DEF AND ULTRA HIGH-DEF RESOLUTION MEDIA)...

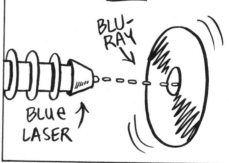

..ARE ACCESSED VIA (YOU GUESSED IT!) BLUE LASERS.

BLU-RAY

BLUE LASER

(OR, IN TRUTH, VIOLET LASERS... BUT "BLUE"/"BLU" JUST SOUND SO MUCH BETTER, DOESN'T IT?)

IT SURE DOES!

THOUGH, PHYSICALLY, DVDs & BLU-RAY DISCS ARE IDENTICAL, THERE ARE MANY DIFFERENCES BETWEEN THE TWO FORMATS.

BLU

DVD

ONE OF WHICH BEING THE AFORE-MENTIONED FEATURE OF HOW MUCH DATA CAN BE STORED ON EACH.

SHOVE

DATA

A STANDARD DVD, ACCESSED AS IT IS BY ITS PLAYER'S LOWER GRADE LASER, TYPICALLY CONTAINS 4.7 GIGABYTES (GB) OF DATA.

THAT'S ABOUT TWO HOURS OF A MOVIE.

NOT MUCH.

THERE ARE DOUBLE LAYERED DVDS, BUT EVEN THOSE ONLY CONTAIN ABOUT 8.7 GB OF INFORMATION, OR ABOUT FOUR HOURS OF A MOVIE.

DVD

HA HA HA! PATHETIC!

A BLU-RAY DISC CONTAINS 25GB OF DATA, WHICH MEANS 13 HOURS OF A MOVIE (STANDARD RESOLUTION) OR TWO HOURS OF A MOVIE... AT HIGH-DEF RESOLUTION...

OMG!

BLU-RAY

DOUBLE LAYERED BLU-RAY DISCS ARE CAPABLE OF 50 GB OF INFORMATION, OR 4.5 HOURS OF HIGH-DEF MOVIE MEDIA OR 26 HOURS OF STANDARD-DEF MEDIA...

GNN

RESOLUTION IN THIS CONTEXT IS DETERMINED BY HOW MANY HORI-ZONTAL LINES OF LIGHT EXIST STACKED ON TOP OF ONE ANOTHER ACROSS THE SCREEN...

SNORT!

THERE MIGHT BE 360 (GOOD FOR SMALLER SCREEN DEVICES LIKE SMART PHONES...

LOWER RESOLUTION MEANS LESS DATA AND THUS MORE APPROPRIATE USE FOR SAID PHONE...

ON A BIGGER SCREEN SUCH AS A TV, THE RESOLUTION LOOKS AWFUL AND WILL BLUR)...

GOD DAMMIT!

480 (STANDARD-DEFINITION), 720 (HIGH-DEF) OR 1080 ("FULL" HIGH-DEF) LINES ACROSS THE SCREEN AS REGARDS THE PICTURE QUALITY...

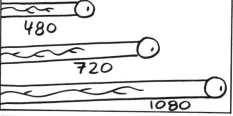

480

720

1080

NOT SURPRISINGLY, THE MORE LINES OF LIGHT, THE CLEARER THE PICTURE.

THEY'RE SO REALISTIC!

I CAN ALMOST TOUCH THEM!

A LOWER RESOLUTION IMAGE MIGHT LOOK SLIGHTLY BLURRED...

ESPECIALLY IMAGES IN THE BACKGROUND

HMM

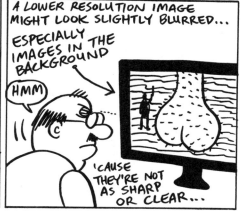

'CAUSE THEY'RE NOT AS SHARP OR CLEAR...

YOU MISS OUT ON SPECIFIC ELEMENTS THAT THE FILMMAKER MIGHT HAVE INTENDED THE VIEWER TO SEE...

WHAT'S THAT SLED SAY? ROSE SOMETHING...?

AND THAT MAY HAVE BEEN EASIER TO SEE ON THE BIG SCREEN THAN AT HOME ON A SMALLER SCREEN.

BLU-RAY REALLY WAS A REMARKABLE STEP FORWARD IN HOME MOVIE VIEWING...

...AS WE COULD FINALLY SEE SO MUCH MORE OF WHAT THE FILMMAKERS INITIALLY INTENDED ON OUR SMALLER SCREENS AT HOME AWAY FROM THE BIG SCREEN THEATERS...

I DIDN'T KNOW WOLVERINE WAS UNCIRCUMCISED...

MAKES SENSE THO...

WE AT MR. SKIN WERE ELATED TO DISCOVER THAT YOU COULD FINALLY ACTUALLY SEE ALL THE WAY IN THERE FOR THAT GLORIOUS UPSKIRT SHOT IN THE SHARON STONE LEG-CROSSING SCENE IN PAUL VERHOEVEN'S "BASIC INSTINCT"!

THANK YOU, BLU-RAY!

CUMMING SOON

LEGACY AND LOOKING FORWARD

A Surprising Skintern of Events

It's still funny to us how many of my employees, even many higher-ups like my president Sam, started off at Mr. Skin as Skinterns, "boob counters," and content technicians pulling and tagging clips. There are plenty of people in content, who are happy working in that department. But you could say it's a rite of passage for those seeking mobility up our pseudo-corporate ladder.

Our designer Doc came to work for us back when we were putting together our second Skincyclopedia volume. He was a literal boob counter, fast-forwarding through movies and TV shows all summer, specifically seeking out breasts to log into our database. *One boob, two boobs, three boobs...more!*

Doc was counting boobs for six months straight, eight hours a day. Talk about *pumping!*

Though it might seem like a dream job to some, Doc—an artist—craved more and started helping out in other ways in the content department. So, Doc was given other tasks, namely searching out, tagging, and cataloging *other* things than just breasts. For four years.

Over time, we realized that Doc possesses extraordinary talent in the realm of graphic design, brought him onto that team, and that's what he's been up to for almost a decade now.

How did Doc end up working at Mr. Skin? He grew up with Sam and my director of operations, Ryan. They were childhood pals. Sam got the job through *another* friend who used to work here in the earliest days. Paying it foreskin, Sam hired on Ryan, who then hired on Doc.

Quick interjection here to say, this is yet another secret of our awesome work atmosphere at Mr. Skin: we often find people through other employees.

"When people do leave Mr. Skin, they want to make sure it stays a cool place to work," Doc says. "So, they'll sometimes help us find someone who will work well here instead of leaving us having to scramble to find some random employee who might end up screwing up the vibe."

It's how we found our ingenious director of business development, James, who buys and sells our advertising for us in the same way Billy Crystal's character does in *City Slickers*. It was almost ten years ago that

James moved to Chicago with his wife and put out the word to local friends asking if anyone knew of any job openings.

"Hey, you gotta call Mr. Skin," someone suggested, so he reached out to us, we brought him in for an interview (and some free food), and now here he is as one of our top-notch team members helping us make even more money than we would have ever conceived of previously.

Jesse, the director of operations for my radio prep branch, is another employee who first came on as a specialized Skintern. He's my wife's cousin—she even used to babysit him!

So, you know how he got *his* job. But, don't misunderstand: Jesse's a very smart, very hardworking person who was in fact studying up for the bar exam when he was starting for us. Anyone can tell you that the bar exam, which allows for a young lawyer to practice in a given state, is one of the toughest certification tests you can take. It's also almost prohibitively expensive, considering the books and classes one needs to prep for it, not to mention the extremely high cost of taking the test itself.

Jesse needed a part-time job to supplement his living expenses while he worked on passing the bar, so the Skintern gig was an ideal situation for him. This was 2007, right around when *Knocked Up* came out, so as Jesse remembers it, this was a "chaotic time" at the company, "but *good* chaos." There was a *lot* to do, and we needed dedicated people like Jesse to come in and take on some of the extra work.

He became one of our main TV Skinterns, going through all the nudity on TV, which at the time was also going through its own "good chaos" with huge shows integrating nudity into them more and more, like HBO's super-sexy vampire series *True Blood*.

"It actually suited me very well," Jesse says. "It was a bunch of busy work for me to do. It was a series of little projects tagging pictures for nudity or cropping box covers for the site. Things like that. I wouldn't call it 'mindless,' but it was stuff that I didn't have to bring home with me at night when I needed to study for the bar without distraction."

Jesse did end up becoming a licensed attorney and remains one to this day, doing some pro bono work on occasion. But, I know what you're thinking: "So, how is Jesse *also* the director of operations for a branch of Mr. Skin?"

NAKED FEAR: WHY HORROR MOVIES CONSISTENTLY SCARE UP SKIN

Aside from out-and-out sex flicks, horror shrieks high as the cinematic genre that can most frequently be counted on to showcase female nudity.

Allow me to play (one-armed) armchair shrink here and propose that it's because vulnerability lays at the core of so many fright flicks, and humans are never more defenseless against attack than when we're unclothed—especially if you're a naked nubile who's suddenly boobs-to-blade against a hockey-masked slasher.

Of course, the opposite can also prove true, in the case of naked knockouts to psycho slayers who use their unexpected, out-of-place nudity as the first means of paralyzing their prey. Think of Mathilda May in *Lifeforce* and Natasha Henstridge in *Species*.

Then, in what I consider the ultimate horror movie for nudity, *Embrace of the Vampire*, Alyssa Milano busts out her boss rack as the victim while Charlotte Lewis vamps it up topless as a boob-hungry bloodsucker.

This bare-meets-scares formula dates back to the earliest iconic horror hits, such as in *King Kong*, when the mighty ape peels off Fay Wray's wrappings like she's a ripe blonde banana; and *Psycho*, where Janet Leigh's taboo-slaying shower exposure climaxes with the mad knife-jabs of Mrs. Bates.

Since then, every era has conjured its own array of hair-raising hotties, from vintage cult-flick scream queens like Linnea Quigley (*Return of the Living Dead*) and Barbara Crampton (*Re-Animator*), to more modern skincarnations such as Sheri Moon Zombie (*The Lords of Salem*). So wherever terror goes, it's clear, toplessness will always follow.

Answer: After all that money and time and energy Jesse spent on the bar exam, not to mention law school before that, even after passing the test (*seriously, not an easy task, folks!*), he decided to stay on at our company, where he climbed into the position he's in today, more than a decade later.

No one can compete for best "secret identity" at the company like our creative director Dan, though. He's one of the few people who came in to essentially do what he's doing for us today. Dan has been here for almost a decade and in that time never worked as a Skintern or in the content department.

He came in as a designer, worked his way up to senior designer, and then became the boss of it all as creative director, overseeing the aesthetic of the site, as well as the visual aspects of some of our newer sites, blogs, and entities we've recently either purchased or created under our Mr. Skin umbrella.

So, you see? You don't *have* to watch nude scenes all day at Mr. Skin to make your way up the ladder!

Dan's nickname around the office is "Ripper." Why? Because he's long been part of a hard-core metal band called Bongripper. (Don't ask.) The funny part is what he's *also* been called in the past: part of "Oprah's Favorite Family."

Yes, *that* Oprah. When Dan and his brothers were younger, Oprah Winfrey would go over to their house to babysit them. You can look this up. It was a segment on her show: "Oprah's Favorite Family."

When she was retiring from her show, Oprah had Dan and his family back on for one of her "Where Are They Now?" specials and showed Dan as a young man all grown up.

Our Dan. The drummer for Bongripper. With an album called *Satan Worshipping Doom*. And the creative director for Mr. Skin.

We're not sure if Oprah is aware of that last element of Dan's "Where Are They Now?" backstory, but she'll likely never read this book, so he's probably off the hook. All they mentioned on the show about him is that he still lives down the street from his mom.

Just one of the many lovely sweethearts we have working so tirelessly for us at Mr. Skin.

Assembling the Squad

That irrepressible former head writer of mine, McPadden, came to us essentially as a fan. A big fan. Maybe the biggest. (Both physically and metaphorically, but he's been working on the former.)

McPadden was a very specific breed of big, big fan. Impassioned. *Very* impassioned. He *really* wanted us to be the best we could be, even before he came on board to help make that happen.

He was living in Brooklyn at the time, taking the F train to work. It's freezing when he gets out, and he's standing there on the corner, shivering to death, and he can't move. Why? Because he's listening on his headphones to me on one of his favorite radio programs, *The Howard Stern Show*. I'm talking about the Anatomy Awards for the first time. It's 2000.

McPadden couldn't get enough. He was totally enthralled. I'm not sure if he skipped work that day or what, but somehow, he was already off to getting on his computer, checking out our site to find his favorite movie star of all time who you've never heard of, Rainbeaux Smith. She was this seventies cheerleader type, and McPadden's scoping out her nude scenes on MrSkin.com.

"I swear, I almost got weepy," McPadden says. "I was like, 'This is everything I ever wanted. This is the future.'"

As a struggling writer, he had no money but joined our site anyway. He *still* has no money today, but at least now he has a free membership.

Back when people would still use a mouse, McPadden was cranking through our site like the maniac fiend I love him as today. It's also still to this day that we argue over a certain point he always gets riled up about. See, he claims we were missing some important flicks, namely: *H.O.T.S.*, *The Godfather*, and *Saturday Night Fever*.

I disagree. I can't *imagine* that we would've been so blind as to have ignored an American movie classic like *H.O.T.S.* That's a sacred text in the church of celebrity nudity!

McPadden became our own personal Mr. Skin critic, shooting off email after email, feverishly *demanding* that we get these movies and the naked actresses featured in them on Mr. Skin. The dude went so far as to create a fake account so that he could basically troll our message board before the word "troll" was used to describe what assholes like him were doing to our humble little site on the grow.

McPadden was absolutely nuts. I *knew* we had to hire him on. This was how that life-changing decision (for me, for McPadden, and for the company) came to pass:

McPadden was writing for a publication in NYC called *Celebrity Skin*. And, yes, they did at one point sue Courtney Love's band Hole. Namely for the publicity. That's the kind of publication they were. And they were at the same time, ironically, ripping off stuff from MrSkin.com left and right.

I call up McPadden, tell him who I am, and he immediately starts shitting bricks. He's worried I'm going to sue *him*. Instead, I ask him to lunch. I happened to be in his neighborhood.

"So, we meet up," McPadden remembers, "and the first thing I thought was, 'That's Mr. Skin? Holy shit!' Because I didn't realize he was so young. I had no idea what he looked like."

Look, I didn't care that McPadden and *Celebrity Skin* were ripping us off. I liked their style and we ended up having drinks, laughing about it. As McPadden wraps it up: "He got drunk, and then he offered me a job!"

I still can't help but find it ironic that McPadden ended up being the one who more than anyone else contributed the always-be-positive aspect of the Mr. Skin voice that has become such a foundation of what we do on the site.

Sure, McPadden's a heavily tattooed maniac who often seems like he hates everything. But his instinct for kindness in writing reviews for MrSkin.com proved killer. Remember, when he first came on, it was the early 2000s—the era of "snark gone wild" on celebrity gossip sites. Perez Hilton was drawing cum shots on paparazzi pics, and basement bloggers would call MTV pop stars "pigs."

Personally, I've never found this brand of writing/blogging to be funny or worthwhile. Still, given the time period, I'll confess that some of this trendy attitude may have infected our early Mr. Skin editorial.

McPadden then comes over to our operation, and, as he puts it: "I was completely awestruck by the site's content and by Skin's personality. But I did notice that some of the write-ups in those earlier days contained slightly mean-spirited jokes like, 'Put your clothes back on!' and terms like 'double bagger.' I hate that stuff. I'm at the site because I love these women! Don't punish me (or them!) for it!"

McPadden thankfully brought to my attention that he had seen how that snarky approach sank other adult businesses.

"There was one video review magazine that I wrote for where the editor seemed only interested in insulting the actresses we were writing about," McPadden recalls. "That guy proved to be the last editor of

Me and Mike "McBeardo" McPadden: my Head Writer for eleven years and ongoing co-conspirator. He was the best and worst employee in company history—which you can kind of tell just by looking at him.

the magazine, as it went out of business after twenty years. Even more than that, though—the nasty tone did not fit Jim McBride as a person."

McPadden's big decree was that every movie that had nudity must be considered a great movie and every actress bio be written expressly for the guy out there who was in love with that actress.

And, you know something? It's worked.

Put Your Money Where Your Smile Is

At Mr. Skin, everyone knows they can trust me, that they'll be paid correctly and on schedule. This may sound simple enough, but as folks who have been around the block a few times at other media outlets will tell you, it's not always the case these days. Sad, but true.

At Mr. Skin, I take care of my people, because they take care of me. Especially since we're all such close friends who have known each other for so many years.

It's undoubtedly a big reason why I'm able to not only get such talented, hardworking people onboard, but why they stick around as long as they do. It's not only a fun place to work. It's a *reliable* place to work, too.

Even when the shit hit the fan in 2007 and 2008 for the economy, I didn't fire a single person. I asked no one to take a pay cut. Actually, this is the one thing I've written that *is* a lie. Sorry, I *did* cut someone's salary to help offset the inclement economic climate: *mine.*

Some people in my life think I can be *too* nice at times. Like in my earlier years of this job when I had trouble firing employees. There haven't been many at all, but there were a few people who took advantage of their position, didn't pull their weight, or were just not the right fit for our office environment.

There was one guy who came to work for us who mandated that we no longer say "boobs," "tits," or "fun bags" anymore in our reviews online. We were only going to use the words "breasts," "chest," or—*ugh*—"mammaries." True story.

I had trouble even firing *him.* And that was only after people like McPadden and Michelle put enough pressure on me to realize I needed to stop complaining about this uppity British snob (or, as McPadden referred to him, "total douche") who clearly didn't understand what we do at Mr. Skin and respectfully show him the door.

As McPadden has just as respectfully noted, there was some "nakedly insane stuff" going on with certain problem people I was too nice about letting go, fake British accents or not. It's sometimes hard to think about the hundreds of thousands of dollars, maybe millions, that I blew by keeping on staff people who just…*sucked* at their job because I was too much of a wuss to say, "Get *out.*"

I had a tech guy back in the day who was costing me a *lot* of money. Regardless of his huge salary, he would still confidently stroll into the office so late that we'd have to push back our weekly meetings to the end of the day just to align our schedule with his.

Instead of my saying, "Hey, asshole! Get to work at ten in the morning and leave at six like everyone else!", I would keep my mouth shut, thinking to myself, *"Oh, man! He's the only tech guy in the world who can keep our website running, so I better not tick him off!"*

I think the moral of the story, aside from the fact I could have subtitled this book *How to Make Money...Despite Fucking Stupidity*, is that I wasn't only taken advantage of by these people. I *deserved* to be taken advantage of by these people. I didn't have the confidence to run the company the way it needed to be run, the way I run it today. I needed to stop being so wide-eyed and naïve to the harsh realities of the business world.

I think some of this overt niceness could be attributed to my being a Midwest guy. In the manner I'm talking about here, it may have hurt me. But I also think it's done some good for me and for the company as a whole, especially since almost everyone at the office is from this seemingly wholesome "aw, shucks" region.

You've heard of "Midwest Nice"? Like the way everyone is in the movie *Fargo*? "Oh, you betcha!" Just real friendly, down-to-earth people. That's us in the office.

Since I'm from and live in Chicago, I kept the business here all these years. If I had early on taken us to New York or LA, the way so many people have suggested over the years, I don't believe we would have been as successful as we are.

Those are cutthroat worlds out there on the coasts. I really think staying around here led me to finding the many people—also from here or from around here—who ended up being totally cool, dedicated, and loyal guys and gals who helped me build the company from the bottom up. It's just a different breed of people here in the Midwest.

So, maybe I can be or have been *too* Midwest Nice and polite in the past. But, it's had its advantages, too.

Look, back in the early days, I was just some guy who'd go on the radio and get signups to the site however I could in this crazy office, where we were making humongous mistakes left and right.

These days, I'm much better. I'm more professional and take things less personally. I'm married, I have kids. I have fifty employees, and many of *them* have kids. If someone's not doing something right and they're becoming a waste of *our* money, I need to make the right choice and send them on their way for the benefit of the company.

Yes, I do think about how much more money I would have today if I hadn't wasted so much unbelievable amounts of cash on these beginner mistakes. I mean, I never got an MBA. I never even went to business school. I was making all of this up as I went along. Despite my best efforts, though, I've been utterly unable to completely screw this all up.

I met my wife through this. I've met Howard Stern and all these amazing radio people, all these terrific celebrities. All of this has happened because I had the balls to start a business even if I had no idea what I was doing.

I've somehow successfully navigated between my R-rated (or occasionally X-rated) life and my more normal domestic life. Clumsily, but still....

And these twenty years of running the number one celebrity nudity site has taught me a *lot* of invaluable lessons about pop culture, the media, business, and human nature. There are no tax write-offs for life experience.

Everything good in my life has happened because I created Mr. Skin. Even though there's been a ton of screwups, the good does outweigh the bad.

Mr. Skin Gets Enlarged

Something specific I'm looking forward to in the future is how Sam and I continue to work together to leverage the power of the Mr. Skin brand. We've been acquiring more websites, partnering with more like-minded companies, and investing in entities that we think are worthwhile in reaching out to markets that go beyond our flagship Mr. Skin site.

You know that we now run *Naked News*, based out of Toronto. In case you couldn't tell by the name, it's an R-rated news show in which—yes—sexy anchors deliver the news completely naked for what's become an iconic web series.

There's also a site called Fleshbot that we bought a few years ago. It's an adult blog that's been doing fantastic for us.

Heck, we even started up an entirely new site called Mr. Man, after folks at my office kept on me about putting together a site for *male* celebrity nudity, too.

In case you're wondering, just as the many ladies in my office could care less about seeing so many boobs and so much bush all day long, the guys have no issue with all the dicks and hairy asses they must go through for Mr. Man. It's all the same to them: we're equal-opportunity pervs in the office. As one of my content guys said, "A penis is just a penis. Who cares? A butt's just a butt."

Curious about how we decide what ends up on Mr. Skin and what ends up on Mr. Man, considering the brave new world we're in now of shifting gender norms? We're very progressive about the distinction and catalog the performer by how she/she/they identifies himself/herself/themselves. And, you know something? We've never gotten any complaints.

Exhibit how we handled a moment from a scandalous scene on the provocative, award-winning Amazon show *Transparent*. Alexandra Billings is lying down on the bed getting a massage by this guy standing above her, and then she turns over and—boing—*Billings has a cock!*

Since Billings identifies as a woman, we bagged and tagged the clip and screenshots from the scene for Mr. Skin, not Mr. Man. We're respectful of her choice as an actress and as a person. We could have been jerks and placed her on Mr. Man, but why do that?

We take what we do at Mr. Man as seriously as our work over the past two decades at Mr. Skin.

We've even begun adding in Mr. Man categories to a special off-shoot of Anatomy Awards that we call our "Manatomy Awards" (which we've already started arguing about, just like at Mr. Skin). There's "Best Half Chub," "Best Balls," "Best Self-Facial".... We had "Best Upper Beard" (that hair guys get in the tramp stamp region) once, but someone else on the team wanted it to be "Best Upper Mustache." So that caused a silly little fracas; whether it's Skin or Man, we can get extremely passionate about making sure everything is just right!

Sure, the bulk of our bread and butter will always come from the latter, but Mr. Man has its noticeable advantages, too. Mr. Man has become the very best male celebrity nudity site online. It's especially taken off in the gay community. I think something like 98 percent of our Mr. Man users are men (plus or minus 2 percent). So, we're definitely doing something right in attracting new demographics that we may have been missing out on before my team got me to launch this new side of our company.

All these new creations, partnerships, and acquisitions have helped to burgeon our bottom line, financially and in every other way, too.

We've gotten some solid mainstream recognition from media outlets as prominent as the *New York Post* about sites we've bought like What Would Tyler Durden Do? (salacious and satirical commentary on media and celebrity; a no-holds-barred approach to the "bitch and famous") and Last Men on Earth (more satire and photo commentary, voiced by YouTube stars Lex and Matt).

We've also purchased and now operate Egotastic (celebrity gossip and entertainment news), Double Viking (comics, fantasy, gaming, gadgets, cosplay; all the geek culture stuff), and CNdb.com (celebrity nudity database; basically a Mr. Skin-lite meets IMDB; *hey, if they can't beat you, buy 'em!*).

With everything we have going on out there online these days, we're controlling nearly one-hundred million page views a month. Which means that even if you had never heard of Mr. Skin before checking out this book, the possibility you'd already seen *something* of ours online is pretty damn good.

It's been so incredibly rewarding stretching out the power of our brand through some of these Safe For Work partnerships and sites that make sense with our sensibility. It's a way to buy in without selling out. If you'll allow me the cliché. But as Dennis Miller would say, "How does a cliché become a cliché?" (Hint: *It works!*)

Let's Get Social

Sam and I are at the same time figuring out fresh ways to leverage our brand in the social media community. This can be a lot harder than it sounds for a company that straddles the line between "mainstream" and "adult." The big boys like YouTube and Facebook don't want to let us play their reindeer games. Linking to our clips and other promotions through online communities such as these or, say, Twitter, can be nearly impossible. Even when we think something is relatively PG, as soon as we place a video, photo, or link on one of these platforms, they can get flagged and ultimately shut down. Serious headache.

It's in fact one of the main reasons we've been taking on these previously mentioned partnerships, so that we can get around this puritanical online blockade. Even if we can't get as much Mr. Skin material out there through general social media platforms, at least we have these Safe For Work sites that work just fine on YouTube, Twitter, Facebook, and elsewhere.

We also enlisted our own millennial as our social media manager who's fully responsible for our brand presence on these networks. Man, you remember the line about Newman saying "the mail never stops" that I mentioned before in reference to our content technicians? Just imagine what it's like for our social media manager Coco!

She's an average twenty-five-year-old gal whose goal in life is to one day start a nonprofit that will help combat the low self-esteem that can come with social media's darker, negative side. She made her mission very clear when she was interviewing with Ryan and Vera, and they were happy to bring her on board, because—once again—we love having folks here from all walks of life, interests, and passions.

Coco doesn't stop at merely overseeing everything Mr. Skin is involved with on social media. She's responsible for the social media interactions for all our offshoot sites and blogs, too.

Imagine the workload; unlike our content guys, who can go home and be away from their computers for a while, Coco has to keep up with her work even when she's away from the office—to the best of her ability—because the global internet is like Wall Street: *it never sleeps!*

"That's the most difficult aspect of my job," Coco says. "It's *all day long.* But, I do like it, because I'm never doing the same thing, and there's always something new to check out every day. Time management is honestly the biggest part of what I do!"

It's easy for some trouble to bubble up if Coco doesn't respond to an online interaction swiftly enough. You know how fast things can escalate online. The opportunistic outrage mob survives off of making *sure* things get out of hand so they can reap the benefits of traffic.

One time, one of our favorite new stars responded on Twitter to a mention we made of her on one of our podcasts. It happened to be a Saturday afternoon, when Coco was not in the office. Unfortunately, not being in the office didn't mean she could let the tweet go by unaddressed.

Most people know what we're about, and they get that we're just having some fun, saluting what it is they're already putting out there for the world to see with their nudity. But, once in a while, you do have little issues like this pop up, and in this case, it involved a pretty big name with a large audience.

The actress had tweeted something at us like, "Don't you have anything better to do?" Not so bad. And, like I said, we're fans of hers, so we didn't want this to become a larger problem.

Poor Coco is just trying to enjoy her weekend, but as she has said herself, she can't ever be 100 percent off the clock, and though it can be exhausting, this is not only her job but also good practice for what she wants to do in the future with her larger career in social media.

Knowing that even something as minor as what this actress tweeted can quickly gain traction and turn into something unmanageable, courtesy of ever-so-friendly tabloid sites on a slow news day, Coco was on it before there was ever even the slightest risk to our brand reputation.

"Because that's my whole job," Coco explains. "Making sure people don't hurt our brand."

That's the way of social media, though. There's some good and there's some bad. As Coco articulates it, "Social media is the world's biggest double-edged sword." She believes that, on one level, social media can connect people in mobilizing activism. But, on the other hand, it can also lead to some pretty nasty stuff, too. "It's beautiful *and* scary," she says. "At the same time."

In the case of this particular actress, to keep things from getting scary too quick, Coco issued a private DM apology right away through Twitter, which seemed to deflate the moment that blew away into the wind of the rest of the millions of tweets issued over the subsequent hour.

There really was nothing else Coco could do at that specific juncture. All she *can* do is remain vigilant. Which means that if, say, she wants to go to a workout class from 10:00 a.m. to 11:00 a.m., she has to schedule her posts in such a manner that nothing will go out on our socials during that hour. This means a lot of predetermined scheduling on her part. It's a good thing she's young and has so much energy!

Also, Coco's not naïve. She understands that, being the powerful double-edged sword it is, social media and sites like ours are also about allowing users to freely express themselves. If they have something critical to say about, oh, for example, just because it comes up a lot, Amy Schumer, they should be able to talk about that plainly and mostly without restraint.

The trick is, as with everything else we do, finding that fine line. The fine line between allowing people to voice their opinions about Schumer or anyone/anything else, while also making sure they're not getting out of control. There's a discernible difference between someone saying "so-and-so is a big hypocrite!" for something that person may have done in the public forum versus "so-and-so should fucking kill herself." Yeah, that's not cool.

As a brand, we would *never* want people to think we support that kind of language or behavior. Trying to find that line between allowing for expressive engagement of our fans and members and people who just need to take their mindless trolling to other less thoughtful sites/platforms is a primary challenge for Coco. Particularly when she's dealing with more provocative content as she does with Mr. Skin, Mr. Man, and WWTDD?. You don't want to be too saccharine or antiseptic, because then our users will lose interest.

A lot of this depends on Coco, her research, understanding, and experience in being the quality social media manager we know her to be.

Luckily for Coco (and the rest of us), our audience is primarily comprised of those who like to have a good time with all of this. Our members mostly engage with us online by talking about *Porky's* being their favorite movie from the eighties (*hell, yeah!*) and that kind of celebratory discussion. There are obviously some rude people out there, but I think most of them know by now to keep that crap off our platform.

One more thing about all this that is interesting to consider: Coco is basically the voice of Mr. Skin and the rest of our brands across all these social media platforms, and her supervisor is Vera, our managing editor. Both young women.

You have all these people out there who think we might just be a bunch of skeevy *guys* working at the office, and yet here are these two crucial positions—essentially the way our company interacts with the public online—being held by two smart and modern young ladies.

It's sometimes funny to us how you have all these people out there interacting with "us" online and have no idea they're talking most of the time to a twenty-five-year-old girl!

Welcome to the Clubhouse

That content guy of ours, Be, remembers when a major news station I won't mention came to do a piece on us, on our day-to-day operation at the Mr. Skin office. They filmed for hours, conducted a few interviews with my staff, and then disappeared without a trace. Fairly normal behavior for news outlets.

When the segment did air some time later, it was much shorter than we thought it would be...and was totally inaccurate in one particularly egregious way. They cut together the piece in such a manner as to make it appear that we only have *guys* working at the Mr. Skin office.

"Yeah, they treated it like we're only a bunch of men in the basement looking at nudie films," Be remembers of the segment. Which isn't so cool, both because it's wrong, but also because we have so many hardworking women on staff here.

To not show that we have both men *and* women working here is disingenuous on the part of this news outlet in question. But, hey, I get it: It's what a lot of people expect from a site like ours. People who don't understand what we're really all about here. And you can't believe everything you read or even see on the news, especially these days.

We really don't have control over how people are going to talk about us, which is another reason I'm so grateful for how Judd Apatow chose to portray us in *Knocked Up*. We hoped for the best, and he delivered. He poked some fun at what we do, but in the end, it was a tribute to us.

The *National Enquirer* used to hit me up a ton during the first five years I was doing this. Constantly. I started to realize they just wanted me to say something they could twist and use to their advantage, the way so many blogs today are just looking for clickbait headlines to attract traffic. I stopped talking to the *Enquirer*, and they eventually left me alone.

Knowing the way we really are in the office all together and then sometimes seeing that image distorted in various news segments or gossip blogs, or whatever it might be, has made for a tough lesson for a lot of my staff and myself over the years. It's a reason why a lot of people at my company don't even bother to read or watch the news for the most part anymore.

I love that, in reality, we have *so many* different kinds of people working for us at the company. My staff is made up of people of all ages, shapes, sizes, creeds, and credos. You come into the office and you'll see some crazy outfits, crazy hair, tons of tattoos, and people who smoke, enjoy drugs, enjoy drinking, having fun. They're all individuals with only *one* thing in common: they're intelligent, good people. Because we don't hire people who are lazy, and we don't hire assholes (anymore).

My employees are people who might need some time off to tour with their band over the summer (like Dan). Or who need to come in a little later one day, because they have to take their kids to school (like Kristina). Or had a little too much to drink the night before (like...uh, *no comment*). But, as long as they get their work done and handle their business, my attitude is: *do what you want; just don't screw up!*

"It's not like they don't want you to work hard here. Because, if you're not working hard, you're gone," Ian says. "But if you prove yourself at this company, prove that you can do your work and do it properly, if you're polite and respectful, the upper management is going to see that and trust you enough to promote you if you're looking to move up."

It's something else I really look forward to in the future: how my staff and I will continue to collaborate in not only making Mr. Skin and our growing network better, but also in the fun times ahead that we're sure to continue to enjoy together.

"You know what's really cool about Skin," my director of business development James says, "is that over all these years, I've never once seen him get upset. No matter if it's a really stressful moment. *He doesn't get upset!* Never even seen him frown. I don't know how he does it: he carries himself in such a way where you never see him get upset or mad or sad. He's just there, all the time, being himself, being Mr. Skin. Always happy."

I *am* a happy guy—I'm living my dream life—but that observation is not *completely* true. I am definitely good at maintaining my cool, but McPadden remembers at least one time when...that wasn't the case.

"Yeah, there was this one time when Jim lost it," McPadden says. "It was when he finally fired this leech we had on staff who had gone off to Europe to set up some deal that turned out to not even exist."

I told you I was a pussy about firing people back in the earlier years. But this jerk really deserved an ass-kicking, and I gave it to him.

"We had this meeting when we realized this guy wasn't actually doing anything in Europe," McPadden continued. "And Jim screams at him, 'Turn your fucking phone off!' I was like, *holy shit!* And then Jim grilled him: 'Where's the deal? *Where's the deal?* Show me the numbers...*now!*' And I'm telling you, I'm *under*playing the mood. Jim was pissed. I'd never seen him like that before. I've never seen him like that since, either, though."

I like to be easygoing at the office, because if I'm that way, this mentality trickles down to everyone else. They see I'm having a good time, and they'll feel free to have the same kind of experience and help keep that feeling alive throughout the rest of the office.

As a young person at the company, Ian still goes out on the weekend raging on most Friday and Saturday nights with his friends. He loves that we encourage him to come on by the office first to pregame when he's in the area and have a few beers, play some pool, and get amped up for the night ahead. "We just use our key to get in, and it's all good," Ian says, "as long as we don't leave a mess, or else I'll get my ass kicked!"

"There's a lot of pride in being able to be yourself here," Katie, our associate editor and one of the youngest people who works at the office, says. "And being able to come and drink with friends after work is awesome. As long as we're getting our work done, we can have all the fun we want!"

This "home away from home" environment that Ian, Katie, and my other employees—young and old alike—can enjoy is exactly what I've worked so hard to cultivate over the years.

There *was* one time, though—at our fifteenth anniversary party—when Ian showed his age, and we had to kick him and a buddy of his out. They were getting way too rowdy, especially his friend he'd brought

At Skin Central, it's boobs on the computer all day, booze in the conference room all night (okay...only most nights). Just ask these deliriously happy skinployees!

who jumped up on the stage we'd set up, messing around with some of the DJ equipment and just being a total jackass.

The little bastards snuck back in behind our backs, so then we had to kick them out a *second* time. But, it was all good. I've known Ian's parents his whole life (I grew up with his dad), so I can vouch for his being a nice kid who happens to also be a hard worker. That's the most important thing. Hey, kids will be kids.

We can give each other some rather outrageous gifts for our annual Secret Santa, and one year, Vera gave Doc a T-shirt with another employee's (Joe P.) high school yearbook picture on it. Who knows how the hell Vera found his high school yearbook picture. The important part is that this was all about an ongoing joke feud between Doc and Joe P. that's gone on for *years*.

The way it started was a guy who used to work here named Raja wanted to get some T-shirts made with a few of the other employees, because there was a place by our Wicker Park office that made cheap custom shirts.

So, Doc and Raja go to the T-shirt place and get some shirts made. And for whatever reason, Doc decided to get one with Joe P.'s name and phone number on it. Doc just thought it would be a good prank. It became the first shot in a long-running, friendly battle between the two of them.

"Joe knew I was going to get a shirt with his name on it," Doc says. "But the next day, when I came into the office and it also had his *phone number* on it, I could see in his eyes that he was just like, '*What the hell, man?!*' It was great! You could totally see it all over his face. He was so pissed. But then, over the rest of the day, he was cool again. But that's what started it. And now we keep doing stuff like that to each other."

I should add this was in Doc's wilder days, when he was single and would go out all the time like Ian and Katie do now. So, he'd be wearing his shirt at all these bars and clubs, meaning Joe P. was getting a ton of random calls from strangers, day and night.

When Ryan one year got Joe P. a shirt with *Doc's* name and number on it, Joe P. then was wearing *that* all around to get back at Doc.

What would Doc do that could turn up the heat on the fake fracas? He decided to legally change his name to Joe P.'s. First, middle, and last. Just for a month.

"I was really about to do it," Doc promises. "I was going to get a new license and everything. Go the whole extent with it. But then I looked more into it and realized, 'Dude! That's a lot of red tape!' So, I backed out. Joe P.'s got a really dry sense of humor and is pretty low-key, which is probably why I've gone after him like this. But he's also the smartest person I've ever met in my life. We're just opposites: the Odd Couple."

A few months ago, I came into the office to discover this massively oversized cookie on our kitchen counter for us all to partake in at our leisure. An outsider would wonder why the hell the frosting was in the shape of Phil Collins with the words "Happy Birthday" written across it. Well, one of my employees has a massively oversized obsession with the pint-sized singer. We're all *well* aware of this in the office, so another one of my staff thought it appropriate to celebrate Collins's birthday for said employee in style. Delicious style.

State of the Poonion, 2015. Celebrating another sex-cessful year of business at the center of my Skinployees.

"Everybody knows each other so well," Be continued. "You're not just some guy in the cubicle next to someone else, or some girl who works up front. You're part of a second family. You're *somebody* here, you know? It's the culture that Skin cultivates; he's a nice guy, talks to you, he knows you, he'll bust your balls to have some fun with you, he'll bring lunch to us, so we can all hang out together and enjoy a great meal. It's one of the great things about who Skin is and it's how he runs the entire company."

The welcoming feeling of family is definitely contagious. Because James can be so focused on his work in business development on his own, he likes to take time to reach out to his fellow staff members when he can, just to check in and say hi. He doesn't have to do it. In fact, it's probably sometimes something he has to go out of his way to do. But, it's important for him that everybody else in the office feels a part of the business side of Mr. Skin.

"I can get into my own world sometimes, riding on a sail, trying to make something happen," James says. "Nobody else might know what I'm up to, so I'll stop into everyone's offices and say, 'Hey, today was good! We really made some money!' Then I'll ask them about how their day went, too. It's just little things like that that helps everyone feel like they're involved."

The Family that Skins Together

I mean it when I say that the Mr. Skin team is a family. You already know about my wife's cousin Jesse and my sister Kristina, both on staff. But, what about *Mom*?

Yup, my mom works for us remotely as a Skintern based out of her home in Arizona. She does some data entry work for us and is also part of our content department, tagging and cataloging clips and photos.

I say you haven't lived until your eighty-year-old mother sends you an email asking, "Is this a bush or a shadow?"

Yes, that really happened. Another way Apatow really got into our heads in the scene when Katherine Heigl's and Seth Rogen's characters experience almost exactly the same moment in *Knocked Up*.

It's a family atmosphere here: Company president Sam cradles Baby Christian "CP" at a Mr. Skin Holiday Party.

Mama Skin! For the past 19 years, my mom, Rosie McBride, has worked for me as a Skintern from her home in Arizona. I knew I'd made it the day I received an email from my mother asking, "Is that a shadow or just bush?"

If you think *that's* classic, how about this next bit about my little old aunt, Margie:

Aunt Margie is *really* Catholic. She attends church every single day.

I had just launched the website and I was visiting Aunt Margie in Arizona with Michelle, who I had just started going out with earlier in the year. Michelle can confirm what we saw, which was this adorable little super-Catholic aunt of mine sitting upright, all prim and proper in her chair, reading some magazine that would've made *Playboy* look like the *National Review*.

Michelle and I can't remember exactly what the publication was, but it was one of those extremely hard-core, niche ones like *Juggs*. Aunt Margie was reading the thing because it happened to have an interview with me in it.

It's Mrs. Skin in the making! This is May 7, 1999—the night I first met my beautiful wife Michelle (far left) during a Pete McMurray live broadcast from The Abbey Pub in Chicago. It took a while for true love to bloom, but how can you resist a guy in a Hawaiian shirt and a sport coat with no money?

How she got a copy, I'll never know. I'll never ask. But there she was, reading my interview, just beaming with pride.

"Oh, Jim!" Aunt Margie swooned. "This is so wonderful. I'm so proud of you!"

Michelle still recalls having trouble witnessing the image through her eyes that were absolutely streaming with tears of laughter. She only wishes she had an iPhone back then so she could have taken a picture of tiny Aunt Margie in her chair, reading some super-hard-core magazine and smiling like her dear nephew had won the Nobel Peace Prize.

I mentioned a while back that my radio booking guy Pete is one of my longest-running and closest friends. I don't mean this only because of everything he's done for us since before Mr. Skin was even a company.

Being friends with Pete also led me to meeting my wife.

We still have a video of that first night when Michelle and I met. That's right: How Mr. Skin is *that*?

Pete was having an anniversary party for his radio show and had invited all these local radio people. A newly anointed member of that community myself, I came and brought...someone other than Michelle.

Michelle was *friends* with my date for the night, though, and agreed she'd show up too, as moral support for her friend. As long as, in Michelle's words, "my friend would promise that I could be a fly on the wall while she told her dad what her latest boyfriend did for a living. It was the most fucking ridiculous thing I had ever heard of in my entire life!"

Once we were all at the party together, it became fairly obvious fairly quickly that Michelle's friend and I weren't really hitting it off. And that Michelle and I *were*.

It was at this place on the north side called Abbey Pub. Pete's on stage, bringing different people up with him, eventually pulling me on along with other big-name celebrities. Like Cindy Crawford! Well, no. But Cindy Crawford's *mom* was there. It was a blast.

I was really working the room, despite Pete's memory of my wearing one of my trademark Hawaiian shirts (three buttons open all night) with white V-neck shirt and (he wants to be clear about this) a zit on my face. I was also apparently "very sweaty."

Despite the fact that I was being bombarded as usual by people trying to stump me with Mr. Skin trivia, Michelle continued to hang around with me, believing the whole time that what I was doing was "the stupidest thing ever." Somehow, stupidity or not, Hawaiian shirt, zit, and flop sweat or not, Michelle found me irresistible and the feeling was mutual. I owe Pete for indirectly introducing me to my wife of almost two decades and mother of my three beautiful children.

When CBS cleaned house in 2005, Pete and his show got the broom. I asked him to come on and book radio full-time for me, and he agreed. He never left. That was fifteen years ago.

Whoa-man!

The future is always happening around us, and as you know by now, we do everything we can at Mr. Skin to keep up with the continually changing times.

We're obviously all very cognizant of the noticeable shifts in the culture these days. Being such a diverse group of people with such varied niche interests, we're not so caught up in our work and hours upon hours at the office each day to lose sight of what's happening outside our doors.

I personally think these changes are a good thing, be they having to do with technology, communication, or vibrant cultural movements.

There's a sincere exuberance in our tribute to the many actresses and female filmmakers who have been making such giant leaps to gain their own agency in entertainment and media over the past years.

WOMEN'S RIGHTS! TOP FIVE NUDE SCENES FEATURING ONLY A RIGHT BREAST

5. **Fran Drescher**—*Cadillac Man* (0:07)
4. **Betsy Brandt**—*Masters of Sex* (S2, Ep12)
3. **Amy Schumer**—*Snatched* (0:29)
2. **Julia Roberts**—*Pretty Woman* (1:35)
1. **Virginia Madsen**—*Class* (0:20)

How sensational did Academy Award-winner Marisa Tomei look when she got topless in 2008's *The Wrestler*? How often do you see a forty-two-year-old woman go bare like that in a movie or TV show? I think it's *awesome* that Tomei chose to be so raw in that incredible film, as do my tireless staff members working so hard to promote her work to our scads of fans across the internet.

There are obviously a few things we've had to consider over the last two years or so, along with so many other companies involved in the entertainment and media industries.

We first thought about holding back some of the promotional reach of our Anatomy Awards in 2018, because there were so many important questions being asked via large platforms about how sexuality was employed in films and television following the backlash against massive figures in the business, like mega-producer Harvey Weinstein.

We wanted to be mindful and respectful of the collective discussions being had around the country and even the world. So, we did little things like not feature in the awards a certain actress we at Mr. Skin all love and admire but who was particularly vocal about the Weinstein backlash. Just in case, as can still sometimes happen as per the tweet Coco had to deal with from that certain unnamed actress mentioned earlier, it could be taken the wrong way.

We had been planning to send out our own silly statuettes to actresses and actors who won our awards, but decided to not risk any complications that could potentially arise with that premise either, and nixed it.

Another understandable question that popped up was whether Howard Stern was going to have us on to promote the awards that year. In the end, though, we went out strong on his program as we always do, and it was a fantastic segment.

Why didn't people freak out about us on *Howard Stern* talking about our Anatomy Awards when so much of the rest of the industry was holding back out of fear of triggering the wrong element? Because, once again, most people know us, they understand us, they get what we do at Mr. Skin. They appreciate our tongue-in-cheek, playful quality and are aware we're ultimately coming from a decent place when we do things like our Anatomy Awards.

And we receive praise for doing what we do by many of the stars we showcase.

Baywatch's Alexandra Daddario is a big supporter of Mr. Skin who feels lifted up by what we do. After she became a fan favorite on our seasonal "Whack-It-Bracket," Daddario publicly announced, "Wow, what can I even say? To all the men who've ever turned me down, now all you can do is look at photos and cry the salty tears of regret."

Anna Paquin is a Mr. Skin fan too, thinks what we do is awesome, and at one point tweeted, "I have nothing but love for Mr. Skin. They celebrate female nudity on film/TV and never say anything mean! What's not to love?"

This especially made Vera excited, because she's a huge fan of Paquin and her show *True Blood*.

Sarah Silverman went to the trouble of writing an acceptance speech after she won her Anatomy Award for "Best Sex with a Teddy Bear" (beat *that*, Independent Spirit Awards!) for her uncharacteristic and astonishingly dramatic performance in *I Smile Back*: "Thank you so much! I am so honored. Masturbating with my [character's] five-year-old daughter's teddy bear in the same room in which she is sleeping was the healthiest choice I've made in years. *L'chaim!*"

Sarah's sister Laura reached out to us when a movie she was in also received some Mr. Skin love: "Holy shit! Our movie *Midnight Sex Run* won a Mr. Skin Award! So excited and honored to be in such great company—yay!"

Ashley Hinshaw, Eva Amurri, and Erin Marie Hogan have all been vocal about their appreciation for our spotlighting them on Mr. Skin.

My wife has a story about this kind of thing involving a well-known actress she grew up with. At one of the cancer foundation events that she helped coordinate, Michelle sidled up to this particular actress friend, who also happened to be there helping, and confessed quietly, "You know, I've got to clear the air…You do know what my husband does, right?"

To which the actress replied, "Oh, yeah. My vagina is *all over* that site!"

Well, I guess that settles that!

If the fact that these ladies are fans of Mr. Skin surprises you, understand that they're not alone in their accolades. I went to the Tribeca Film Festival one year and ran into documentary filmmaker Michael Moore, who confessed his gratitude for what we do on the site, too.

Andy Richter has tweeted out his love for us in the past, and Jimmy Kimmel gave us a really sweet blurb for the back cover of one of our Skincyclopedia books. Speaking of, we once saw an interview with Ben Stiller where we could all see in the background, clear as day and right there on his bookshelf, a Skincyclopedia of his own. Thanks, Ben!

But I think the *most* surprising praise came from the guy who took over for Siskel & Ebert, Mr. Richard Roeper himself, who said it best: "Mr. Skin knows more about nudity in the movies than any person who ever lived has ever known about any subject. Ever."

"GILBERT NUDITY"

Gilbert Gottfried is not just one of the funniest comedians to slay from a standup stage, as a longtime voice actor for cartoons, and onscreen in TV and film (who can forget his recurring role as, well, basically himself in the *Problem Child* movies?). He may also be even more obsessed with naked women than I am—which *is* saying something (in the famous "Gilbert voice," of course).

On top(less) of all that, Gilbert has become one of the best podcasters in the game. In 2015, it was amazing and colossal indeed when I heard Gilbert and guest Paul Shaffer discussing Mr. Skin and how I "fast-forward to the good parts."

It was even more of a blast when I visited the podcast myself and learned about "Gilbert Nudity"—which is what the funnyman calls his favorite form of naked movie moments, in which an actress appears doing everyday tasks in the nude.

- **Blanchard Ryan**—*Open Water*. Bodacious blonde Blanchard bares boobs and bush while reading in bed.
- **Karen Gillan**—*Not Another Happy Ending*. Karen treats us to side-nip and butt-crack while typing at a computer in the buff.
- **Kether Donohue**—*You're The Worst* (S3, E12). Volcanically voluptuous Kether will have you following an appendage other than your nose as she noshes on Fruit Loops while naked.

What's really exciting for my staff and me is how so many women are now producing an incredible spate of their *own* shows and movies in which they'll often feature actresses or even themselves as totally bare to the world.

Lena Dunham *chose* to present herself naked on *Girls*. She might not be the most conventionally attractive woman, but she said, "Fuck it; let's do this!" Just like with Kathy Bates before her, we never fat-shamed or slut-shamed Dunham, as so many reviewers and critics have in the past. We were like, "This is great! You go, Lena! We all love it at Mr. Skin!"

You have Frankie Shaw's own show *SMILF*, in which she plays a horny single mother trying to raise a kid. Shaw writes, directs, and created the series that we can't get enough of at the office, especially when she shows off that seductive body of hers.

Be Sirius! With the amazing, colossal(ly horny) Gilbert Gottfried at the taping of his 100th podcast at SiriusXM. "Gilbert Nudity" forever!

How about Issa Rae's *Insecure*? A black woman who writes, directs, and stars in her own series and chooses to put nudity in all the time? Beautiful.

It's so cool to us at Mr. Skin that these women are calling the shots now. They can't be pushed around. They're the boss. The buck stops with them. They're making the big money on these shows, and we will continue to celebrate such needful changes.

How fantastic is it that more established, seasoned women like Madonna can still strut their stuff and make headlines with wild antics, too? Here's a woman that—even after having taken over the world multiple times over the past four decades—can keep using her sexuality as a tool for power.

Remember when Madonna said she'd give a blowjob to anyone who voted for Hillary Clinton in the 2016 election? And that she *swallows*? Here is a woman using her own sexuality in an attempt—even in jest—to get the leader of the free world elected! *That's* power. *That's* what we're celebrating at Mr. Skin!

In case you think this is a lot of PR hype or lip service, I'll tell you I do put my money where my mouth is. In fact, appropriately enough, I'll give the floor to Michelle on this one:

"Jim's this amazing man who supports women, supports women's rights, supports the right to choose, and *vehemently* supports equal pay for women. So, he talks about boobs? So, he talks about people getting naked in movies? There's nothing *wrong* with boobs or laughing about boobs or finding boobs sexy. That's why they're in the movies in the first place!"

Skinto the Future

And *speaking* of boobs, the amount of nudity they're showing in the movies and series these days is spectacular, too. Stuff we would have *never* seen five or ten years ago.

I think a lot of this started with Dunham's *Girls*, actually. Some people remember where they were when Kennedy got shot or the first man landed on the moon. I remember the historic moment in television history when we saw semen on the small screen for the first time with Adam Driver giving Shiri Appleby a pearl necklace. *It's not TV! It's HB-BLO!*

That had never happened before in the history of television in such a graphic sexual context. You hardly see such a blatant use of spooge even in movies, aside from the memorably funny scenes in *There's Something About Mary* and Todd Solondz's dark comedy *Happiness*.

There was a quick moment of squirt in *Sex and the City* once, back in the early 2000s, but never like what we saw on that episode of *Girls*. Or what we later saw in an episode of *Insecure* where a guy Rae's character was fellating blows a load into her face. Or, wait. Let me rephrase: *He blew a load all over her face.* That's been previously unheard of on TV.

On an episode of *SMILF*, Shaw's character is having sex with some guy who she's giving a blowjob to, and he shoots his load into his *own* face!

The level of graphicness in this stuff is mind-*blowing*.

Was there any more momentous occasion in the history of television nudity than when *Girls'* Allison Williams gets her ass eaten out in Season Five?

I'm sure I don't have to go into how wild *Game of Thrones* can get with its nude scenes. And here we go again: It's not *porn*. It's not even NC-17 much of the time. It's totally mainstream, out-there-to-the-masses pop culture that everyone's watching, talking about, and giving award after award to.

In the first episode of the second season of *High Maintenance*, Natalie Joy Johnson is having sex with two guys at the same time. And not in the traditional manner you're used to seeing on the Hallmark Channel or in the aisles at your local Walmart. No. We're talking one guy eating her out and the other munching on her butthole.

How's about *Snowfall?* You have this show that's not even on premium cable—it's totally commercial television with ads and everything—on FX. (Owned by Fox! Rupert Murdoch! Hilarious.) It's this captivating series based in the 1980s, in which they have an episode where a guy ends up fucking this girl—his naked ass, her naked ass—and she's blowing coke up his butthole with a straw, and then he ODs.

This was on *commercial TV, man!* Not in a movie. Not on cable. Not online. This is the future of nudity onscreen. There's no question we're seeing more and more graphic content than we could have ever thought possible before. Even as of five years ago. Now it's a constant flow in which everyone is trying to outdo everyone else. There's simply no stopping it now.

As I write this, there are 137 shows across thirty-five networks that exhibit nudity. And that's not including streaming services. Netflix has twenty-eight shows with nudity in them. Amazon and HBO are tied for twelve. Even my old childhood companion, National Geographic, has a channel that airs a miniseries called *Long Road Home* that features plenty of nudity.

When I first started Mr. Skin back in 1999, there were maybe five shows that had nudity on them with regularity. Now we have 137.

TEN MOST GRAPHIC TV SEX SCENES

Tune in, turn on, get off.

10. **Rayna Tharani**—*The Young Pope* (S1, Ep6)
 9. **Sheena Sakai**—*Power* (S4, Ep5)
 8. **Natalie Joy Johnson**—*High Maintenance* (S2, Ep1)
 7. **Ivana Milicevic**—*Banshee* (pilot ep)
 6. **Laura Niles**—*Californication* (S1, Ep10)
 5. **Alice Henley**—*Rome* (S2, Ep9)
 4. **Mishele Prada/Michelle Badillo**—*Vida* (S1, Ep3)
 3. **Michelle Borth**—*Tell Me You Love Me* (S1, Ep8)
 2. **Karley Sciortino**—*Easy* (S2, Ep3)
 1. **Allison Williams**—*Girls* (S4, Ep1)

I can't wait to see what comes up next in the years ahead. How far will this all go? What else can they conjure up that we haven't seen yet? There's some *stiff* competition among all these networks, cable channels, and streaming services. So, we know it's gotta be good.

For those wondering if *I* have my limit on what I'd watch, let me just say, "Not really." More or less. (*No shit.*)

It's such an exciting time to be alive, watch it all progress, and be part of the action in my own small but enduring way.

CGI T&A

"Fake News" has nothing on today's Fake Nudes.

When Mr. Skin launched back in the late '90s, Computer Generated Imagery (CGI) was a relatively new technology and, in Hollywood terms, remained in the domain of sci-fi epics and action blockbusters.

In the two decades since then, it seems like everything is now computer-generated—and that includes, believe it or not, movie and TV nude scenes. While that's a buzzkill for naked celebrity fans, just think about the devastation this has posed to the once-bustling Body Double industry!

Early on in this digital revolution, the sexperts at the Skin Labs could easily spot bogus breasts and ersatz ass created by keyboards, but now, as the technology continuously evolves, it's getting tougher all the time.

In 2011, *The Change-Up*, a raunchy comedy co-starring the lovely Leslie Mann, made us realize just how daunting the CGI nudity challenge was destined to become.

At the forty-six-minute mark, Leslie pops open her top to reveal a sizable pair of buoyant bare boobs that appear to be perfect. In fact, they're just a bit too perfect, and that's what prompted the Skin Labs to skinvestigate in full.

From there, we visually determined that Leslie's on-screen lacto-orbs were too big for her body frame and too gravity-defiant to even be implants. On top of that, no way was the real-life Mrs. Judd Apatow suddenly busting out her Apa-two on film. We made the call and we were correct: the true age of CGI T&A had arrived.

WRECKED BY TECH: FIVE EVIL CGI NUDE SCENES

Do not be fooled: any flesh you think you see here is a synthetic simulation perpetrated by pure computer trickery.

5. Jessica Alba—*Machette* (0:37)

4. Charlotte Gainsbourg—*Nymphomaniac: Vol II* (0:24)

3. Leslie Mann—*The Change-Up* (0:46)

2. Marian Cotillard—*Ismael's Ghosts* (0:56)

1. Lena Heady—*Game of Thrones* (S5, E10)

I'm knocked out by how celebrity nudity has upped its game over the last few years. This is perhaps the most significant reason of all why Mr. Skin can thrive during a time when there's so much free nudity online and elsewhere: there is such a glut of nudeness in mainstream flicks and TV that *someone* has to keep up with it, track it, organize it, and present it in entertaining and informative ways for the clamoring public at large.

And that someone is us! It's me! Mr. Skin!

I don't know if I'll ever fully be able to get over the fact that *this* is what I get to do with my life. That I get to come into the office every day and lead this incredible group of amazing people who support me and

Michelle and I smile alongside Jimmy Kimmel at the 2013 charity event, Variety Power of Comedy. Jimmy once said of me: "I no longer have to waste valuable time with plot. More than just a timesaver, Mr. Skin may have saved my life."

are my friends and even a few family members there to work their asses off with me, sharing some boisterous laughs along the way.

I can't believe that I could go from some horny teen taping nudie scenes from random, rare seventies movies on my two Betamax players to being Mr. Skin.

Which brings me right back to where I started. *Do I have the best job in the world?* Well, I've been totally honest with you up to now, so I might as well say it and say it proud: *Hell, yeah, I do!*

MR. SKIN'S FAVORITE NUMEROUS NUDE STARS

The most skintastically prolific peelers in skinema history.

5. **Susan Sarandon**—16 Nude Appearances
4. **Marion Cotillard**—18 Nude Appearances
3. **Nicole Kidman**—19 Nude Appearances
2. **Sharon Stone**—21 Nude Appearances
1. **Monica Bellucci**—27 Nude Appearances

MY TOP TEN FAVORITE NUDE SCENES OF ALL TIME

Mr. Skin's personal picks for the most arousing of all on-screen exposures:

10. **Group shower scene**—*Porky's* (1:02)
 9. **Eva Green**—*The Dreamers* (0:50)
 8. **Jennifer Connelly**—*The Hot Spot* (1:26)
 7. **Adele Exarchopolous/Lea Seydoux**—*Blue is the Warmest Color* (1:20)
 6. **Mimi Rogers**—*Full Body Massage* (1:05)
 5. **Sharon Stone**—*Basic Instinct* (0:27)
 4. **Halle Berry**—*Monster's Ball* (1:13)
 3. **Alexandra Daddario**—*True Detective* (S1E2)
 2. **Kelly Preston**—*Mischief* (0:59)
 1. **Phoebe Cates**—*Fast Times at Ridgemont High* (0:51)

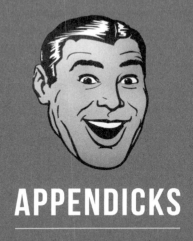

APPENDICKS

Cast of Characters

Be – Content Tech. Joined the Content team in 2013 to work on the newly launched MrMan site. Local legend as graffiti artist "BboyB." Married to Vera, the managing editor. Loves graffiti, dad jokes, motorcycles, Vera. One of the few people in the office who prefers to talk in person rather than on instant messenger.

Christian "CP" – Video Production Manager. Started in 2008 in the content department. Thanks to music and recording background (plays guitar and drums in bands), took over the position of audio engineer, then moved up to Production Manager in 2017. Gives out gifts at every Secret Santa that feature a picture of himself. Known for wearing hot pants at the holiday party. Practically a saint.

Coco – Social Media Manager. Started at Mr. Skin in October 2017. Applied for the job because she has a background in sex-ed and felt like it was a seamless fit. Loves cooking and writing.

Dan/"Ripper" – Creative Director. Started in 2009. His wife Jackie works for the company, as well. Driving force behind major Skin redesigns. Drummer in the world-famous doom metal band Bongripper. Was once featured on *Oprah* as a child. Loves the Green Bay Packers.

Doc – Graphic Design. Design perfectionist. Positive Vibes Technician. Best hair in the office for the last twelve years. Ran "Doc's Lounge" at all Skin parties. Was the "Blu-ray Ninja," known for finding new nudes in HD. Loves to pull office pranks, especially on tech.

Ian – Quality Assurance Specialist. Makes sure the many site changes are working before launch. Friendliest person in tech. Avid LEGO® collector. Second best drummer in the office.

Jackie – Radio Prep Services. Started in customer support in 2011. Handled the first customer support retention over the phone under the name "Amber." Moved to radio prep services, but now her sister also works in Skin customer support. Real family affair at Skin. Married to Ripper, has one son with him.

Jesse – Radio Prep Services Manager. Started as a Skintern in 2007 while studying for bar exam. Became a licensed attorney, but decided to stay at Skin instead and dedicated a few years to the Mr. Skin content side. Now heads the radio prep business as Director of Operations. Loves Michigan State, too much.

Jim K. – CFO. Wrote actress bios and movie reviews in the earliest days of MrSkin.com while chipping in with the bookkeeping. Over time, became the supreme overlord of all things money as CFO. Loves to ask the tough questions. Skin won't make a business decision without his input. Doles out pun-laden barbs.

Joey – Content Manager. Started as a Content Skintern tagging videos, moved up to Content Tech in 2012, then Content Manager in 2016. Obsessed with organizing and refining workflows. Helps keep Skin skinformed on all the latest nudity. Has two dogs.

Katie – Writer. Joined Skin as a writer in 2015, wanted to work here because of the sex-positive attitude in the office and on the sites. Loves Taco Bell, beer, being positive.

Kristina/"Sister Skin" – Human Resources. Jim McBride's actual younger female sibling, who heads up Human Resources among her other positions at Skin Central. Kristina is #3 in the order of the four original McBride offspring, but forever #1 in the hearts of all who work with her. Smart. Sweet. Sassy. Married mom of two. Literally the last person you'd expect to work for a naked celebrity company—*or* for the big brother who always drove her crazy!

Lisa – Office Manager. Hired in 2014 to manage the day-to-day operations of the office. De facto office mom. Knows everyone's secrets. Will dish out the tough love. Opera singer. Considers singing "12 Days of Titsmas" for Skin a crowning achievement, even after obtaining a Master's in Vocal Performance.

Mike/"Skin Jr." – World's foremost authority on any nude scene that's not in English. Instrumental in establishing the company and our completist approach to skinternational nakedness. Moved on to his own success in various online fields. Tall.

Mike McPadden – Former Head Writer. Did more than anyone beside Mr. Skin to establish the business's tone, identity, and humor, but drove more co-workers insane than anyone else in the process. Hence why he amicably moved on to pursue his freelance career. Author of the second and third greatest books of all time (you're `presently reading #1): *Heavy Metal Movies* (Bazillion Points, 2014) and *Teen Movie Hell: A Crucible of Coming-of-Age Comedies From Animal House to Zapped!* (Bazillion Points, 2019).

Pete – Radio Booker. Radio personality who started working as Skin's booker between on-air gigs, then never left. Has broadcast on seemingly every station in Chicago. Loves to talk, loudest person in the office. Skin's biggest fan. Says he'll never leave now that we have a kegerator and free peanuts.

Ryan – Director of Operations. Started as a Skintern in spring 2004, after returning from teaching English in Japan. Thought he was going to stay at Skin for a short while before moving to South America to teach English again. Fourteen years later is still here. All Skin work projects flow through him. Used to be the last man standing at all Skin parties. Married with two kids (thereby explaining the "used to be" in the last sentence).

Sam – President. Started working at Skin as his first real job after graduating from college. After almost eighteen years, he's spent nearly half his life so far working for the company. He now runs the business side of Skin. Work is a big part of his life, and the rest is devoted to family: married with three kids. Amazing networker, knows everyone, everywhere.

Vera – Managing Editor. Started as a freelance writer in 2011, promoted to Managing Editor in 2012. Married to Alberto "Be." Even keeled. Even steven. Most frequently described as "normal," once "intensely normal." Mentored many a young writer on how to churn out boob puns.

Skinfinitions

Anatomy Awards: Mr. Skin's annual one-armed salute to the very breast in the previous year's nudity in film and television. We've been polishing those trophies since 1999.

Backburger: Bush seen from behind. See also: **Rear Burger**

Body Double: A professional naked stand-in whose stunt privates substitute for a star who's too skingy to perform a nude scene herself.

Braille Nips: Babes with bumps on their areolas.

Breast Sizes:
- **Small:** Taut and tiny: more nip than knocker. Sunken treasures and carpenter's dreams who flat-out beautify the Itty-Bitty Titty Committee. (Goldie Hawn, Nastassja Kinski)
- **Medium:** A happy handful of hooterage.
- **Large:** C-cups and upward to delectable double-Ds.
- **Jamambo:** Monstrously massive, all-natural mountain-sized mammaries. Note: Jamambos are always referred to as "jugs"— not breasts, not hooters, not nay-nays. Always: Jugs.

Caged Monkey: Pubic hair that sticks out the sides of bikini bottoms or underwear. See also: **Larry Fine**, **Oscar Gamble**

Cheek Peek: Sometimes accidental—and sometimes definitely not— exposure of the bottom-most buttocky seat-meat.

Down-Blouse: An inadvertent overhead peek into the confines of a starlet's shirt, oftentimes resulting in a nip-slip.

Eyeful Towers: Big French breasts.

Fire on the Hole!: Naturally red pubic mound.

Full-Frontal Nudity: Simultaneous naked exposure of both breasts and pubic mound in the same shot.

Furburgerage: Hair, beautiful hair, of the pubic persuasion.

Hardwood Floor: Bald-shaven female crotch.

Iceberg Boobs: Breasts peaking up out of water, with the nipples acting as the "tips."

Itty Bitty Titty Committee: Unofficial support organization for the bite-sized-breasted beauties worldwide who, ironically, don't need much support up top.

Larry Fine: Pubic hair that sticks out the sides of bikini bottoms or underwear. See also: **Caged Monkey, Oscar Gamble**

Lesbianism: Any on-screen sensual contact from kissing and canoodling to full on cunnilingus between two women. Or more, if we're lucky.

Lip-Slip: An accidental, momentary revelation of an actress's labia.

Lobster Girl: All the meat is in the tail.

Marty Feldman Boobs: Breasts that have nipples pointing in the opposite directions, much like the famously frazzled bug eyes of the late British funny man from *Young Frankenstein*.

Mashed Potato Boobs: Everything tanned but the boobs.

Mufftastic Muff: Lush, long, fluffily grown-out pubic hair of the sort women typically sported prior to the 1980s.

Nip-Slip: An accidental, momentary revelation of the best part of the breast, typically from an open blouse or a deep plunging neckline.

Niptastic Nips: Extra-long, deliciously thick, toweringly tall boob-spigots.

Nudecomer: A first-time flesh-flasher.

Oscar Gamble: Pubic hair that sticks out beyond the edges of underpants or bikini bottoms, in this case specifically that of an African-American actress or other cocoa-hued beauty. See also: **Caged Monkey, Larry Fine**

Plumber's Crack: Accidental exposure of the butt crack above the waistline of pants or skirt, especially from bending over.

Pressed Ham: A bare butt smushed up against see-through glass.

Pressed Mams: Bare boobs smushed up against see-through glass.

Public Nudity: Any exposure of the nipples, butt, pubic hair, or labia in an outdoor setting where passersby are likely to witness the revealed body parts.

Racktastic: Breast-intensive.

Rear Burger: Bush seen from behind. See also: **Back Burger**

Robo-Hooters: Surgically augmented breasts with unmistakable implants. AKA—Plastic Fantastics.

Skiing/Ski Poles: A three-way sex act wherein a woman places herself between two men and, at the same time, manually manipulates their he-handles.

Skingoria: Knockout nudity and blood-soaked violence in the same scene—where flesh and blood collide!

Skingy: It rhymes with "stingy" and means the same thing: an actress who is not generous when it comes to doing nude scenes.

Skinterracial: Naked on-camera sexual contact between members of different races.

Swingers: Hefty breasts so positively pendulous that when we see an actress disrobe from behind, the backs of her bombers bobble clearly into view.

Teeter Totter: Three-way sex with a man laying flat on the bottom, one female atop his face and the other riding his rod, thereby approximating the appearance and motion of a see-saw.

Turkey Timer Nipples: Hard nips through a shirt.

Up-Skirt: An unexpected peek between the thighs of a dress-clad starlet.

Best of "Heard at Mr. Skin"

We recently realized at Mr. Skin that some of the things that get said, discussed, and messaged internally on Slack back and forth between one another at the company are pretty fricking funny. So, we started up a Twitter page literally called "Heard at Mr. Skin."

Here now are five of our favorite such tweets. All of these are things we've actually said and overheard in the office.

 Heard at Mr. Skin
@heardatmrskin

" I was wondering if I should change the rating of this scene from 4 to 3 stars since the breasts are covered in alien make up?"

2:09 PM · 07 Mar 16 ·

 Heard at Mr. Skin
@heardatmrskin

Actual statement from our editorial group chat:
"I asked my friend who was invited to swanberg's sex party for more details and she told me there was pizza at it."

This is just too much eroticism to handle.

2:18 PM · 28 Jun 18 ·

Heard at Mr. Skin
@heardatmrskin

"do you think @JergensUS stock just skyrocketed the day mrskin.com launched?" #moisturize

4:58 PM · 08 Apr 16 ·

Heard at Mr. Skin
@heardatmrskin

[Redacted] uploaded a file: "erection_stuff.zip"

10:17 AM · 06 Sep 16 ·

Heard at Mr. Skin
@heardatmrskin

"To me, 'bush' sounds sexier. 'Pubes' is like something you find on your sandwich."

4:10 PM · 04 Feb 16 ·

T&ACKNOWLEDGMENTS

Jim would like to thank Anthony Ziccardi from Post Hill Press for publishing this book.

He also gives supreme thanks to all who ever worked at MrSkin.com these twenty years. Each has contributed in some way to making this book possible.

A special thank you to Jim's crack skin-house content team, Marilu Ramirez Castro, Eric Braband, Sam Westerling, Alberto "Be" Trevino, and Jason Ogawa for fast-forwarding to the good parts so Jim doesn't have to anymore.

And to his head of content Joey Murphy whose hard work and organizational skills makes Jim's job so much easier…

Thanks to designer extraordinaire Dan "Ripper" O'Conner.

Also photo editor Matt Kimbro.

All of Jim's editorial contributors: Steve Attanasie, Nicholas Kania, Stephanie Weber, and especially Vera Napoleon.

Thanks to Austin Fiascone and Phil Henricks.

Also Doc Heath for all he's done for Jim through the years.

Coco Mertens, social media guru.

Lisa Horwitz, office manager—who does everything for Jim. (Thank you.)

To Jim's techtastic tech team led by Steve Podlecki, and including David Nanry, John Hanson, and Ian Robertson. A special shout-out to the skinternational dev team who work remotely all over the world.

Special thanks to Ryan McClughen, and Jim K., part of the "wet" dream team of SK executives.

To Sam Rakowski who has done a great job as president of the company, especially while Jim's out hawking this book.

And, of course, to Mathew Klickstein and Mike "McBeardo" McPadden. Without them, you'd be reading a pamphlet instead of a book.

And most importantly to Mrs. Skin—Michelle.

MATHEW thanks the team at Foundry Literary for connecting him to the wild world of Mr. Skin and all that has followed. Anthony Ziccardi, Maddie Sturgeon, and the rest of the fine folks at Post Hill deserve ample praise for their tireless and meticulous efforts on this project, as well. Special thanks are due to Matt Fondiler (no pun intended), Mike August, and Adam Carolla for delivering the fantastic foreword.

Mathew as always thanks his friends and family for continued encouragement, support, and wide ears listening to much stressed-out kvetching. Particularly fellow soldier-authors (once again, those poor boys): Caseen Gaines, Allen Salkin, Jon Niccum, Jai Nitz, and Adam Bradley.

An exploiter of the coffee-shop-as-office approach to the work day, Mathew must also thank the dedicated staff at Niwot, Colorado's own Old Oak Coffeehouse, for providing the atmosphere, music, good brew, and comfy tables at which the bulk of his contributions were produced.

Most importantly, he thanks Ellis Henican and Mike McPadden for their constant consultation and friendship throughout the entire process; Johnny Ryan for bringing to life the incredible comix for this book; and, obviously, Jim McBride, Michelle McBride, and the entire gang at Mr. Skin (notably Lisa Horwitz for all the organizational assistance viz. many trips up to Chicago) for their welcoming him into their two-decade adventure that continues onward.

Oh, wait…also the feisty Miranda to his quirky Steve: the wife, Becky.

ABOUT THE AUTHORS

Jim Mcbride (aka Mr. Skin) is the founder and CEO of MrSkin.com and its multimedia parent company SK Holdings. He has appeared on more than five hundred radio shows and lives in the Chicago area with Mrs. Skin and their three children. This is, believe it or not, his third book.

Mathew Klickstein is a writer and filmmaker whose work has appeared in *Wired, NY Daily News, Vulture,* and *The New Yorker.* His previous books include *SLIMED! An Oral History of Nickelodeon's Golden Age* and *Springfield Confidential: Jokes, Secrets, and Outright Lies from a Lifetime Writing for The Simpsons* (with original series writer Mike Reiss). The publication of Mathew's comedic novel about "geek culture," *Selling Nostalgia,* is forthcoming this summer. His films include *Act Your Age: The Kids of Widney High Story, On Your Marc,* and Sony Pictures' *Against the Dark.* And he is the host/co-producer of the interview-based podcast *NERTZ,* based on his book *Nerding Out: How Pop Culture Ruined the Misfit.* Mathew became involved in this sui-generis project after suggesting to his agent that he write a history of Wild Turkey brand bourbon, with his agent asking if he'd instead care to take an assignment floating around the office about Mr. Skin. At the time, Mathew had never heard of Mr. Skin and assumed it was a condom company. www.MathewKlickstein.com

Johnny Ryan is an Eisner Award-nominated comics artist who grew up in Plymouth, MA, near the Pilgrim Nuclear Power Plant. He is the creator of such legendary underground series as *Angry Youth Comix, Blecky Yuckerella,* and *Prison Pit.* His work has appeared in *MAD*

Magazine, Vice Magazine, LA Weekly, Hustler Magazine, The Stranger, and, of course, *Nickelodeon Magazine.* Johnny was, additionally, the co-creator of Nickelodeon's animated series *Pig Goat Banana Cricket.* He now lives in Los Angeles and hopes this gig will get him a lifetime pass to MrSkin.com.